Let's Take 'em Flyin'

A True Story About the Nation's Top
High School Aerospace Science Program

Bill Powley

Let's Take 'em Flyin'

A True Story About the Nation's Top
High School Aerospace Science Program

HISTRIA
PERSPECTIVES

Histria Perspectives

Las Vegas ♦ Chicago ♦ Palm Beach

Published in the United States of America by
Histria Books
7181 N. Hualapai Way, Ste. 130-86
Las Vegas, NV 89166 U.S.A.
HistriaBooks.com

Histria Perspectives is an imprint of Histria Books dedicated to outstanding non-fiction books. Titles published under the imprints of Histria Books are distributed worldwide.

Library of Congress Control Number: 2024944046

ISBN 978-1-59211-511-2 (softbound)
ISBN 978-1-59211-526-6 (eBook)

Contents

This book is dedicated to all those mentioned in the book who have enriched my life and allowed me to have such a wonderful adventure. I am so blessed to have so many families — my biological family, my church family, my military family, my flying family, my education family, my sports family, and my canine family. I am most blessed to have my beautiful, intelligent, dedicated, vivacious, charming, brilliant, loyal, awesome, breathtaking, stunning, astounding, awe-inspiring (hope I got enough adjectives in) wife Phillis, who is literally the wind beneath my wings. I respect and admire all of you.

— Bill Powley

Preface

This is a personal account of my military career, Air Force Junior Reserve Officer Training Corp (AFJROTC) Instructor, and founder of Flight Lesson Instructional Grants Helping Teens (FLIGHT) Foundation. I avoided assignments in the Air Force involving teaching and flight instruction. Upon my retirement in 1991, how ironic that I found great success as a teacher and flight instructor. God has a plan, and apparently, it doesn't matter what we think. This is a fabulous story of teamwork and dedication to build the best aviation high school program in the nation. I am honored to be the leader of the team and to tell the story.

Chapter 1
Bob Gomez
(1967-1970)

April 23rd, 1970 — Ubon Royal Thai Air Force Base, Thailand — 1030 hours. I was in my hooch (room) and either heard my name called or a commotion outside. I stepped out onto a boardwalk in front of the rooms and saw someone coming toward me from about 20 yards away. He yelled out, "Bob didn't come back." The shock of those words caused me to see that picture forever. Someone standing outside their door two rooms down on the left, a pole holding the roof over the boardwalk just in front and to the left of me, and the backdrop of the other hooches and base in the distance. Just like the image I have of where I was when Kennedy was shot, and when the twin towers went down. I was numb and in shock. I don't remember any of the rest of the day except that I went down to the flight line to see if any other information was available and was at the Officers Club (O'Club) that evening with some fellow Wolf Fac's (Forward Air Controllers) who were in a somber mood.

Bob and I had met in church at Reese Air Force Base (AFB) in Lubbock, Texas. He was a class or two behind me, a graduate of the University of Florida. We spent some time together socially with local church members, but other than that we were busy learning to fly T-41s, T-37s, and T-38s. Bill Delaplane, my best friend and roommate at the United States Air Force Academy (USAFA) was the only squadron mate in my pilot training class 69-02.

I have no record of when I soloed. The tradition in pilot training was to throw the solo student into the swimming pool, flight suit and all. I did not start keeping my own personal logbook until after pilot training. Just didn't seem important at the time since the Air Force was keeping track of our time (Form 5).

One of the traditions that Bill Delaplane and I had, along with two or three other students, was to play the pinball machine every day during lunch at the O'Club. We got pretty good at it, and we had a pretty good correlation between how good our flight lesson would go based on how smooth and coordinated our pinball playing was at lunch.

When assignments were picked following graduation, Bill and I both took F-111s to Nellis AFB, Las Vegas, Nevada. There were no F-4s, F-105s, or other fighter assignments. Off to Nellis in October 1968, Bill signed in and I put a deposit down on a house owned by a friend of mine, Norm Wells, an F-4 double Mig killer, and went on leave. Returning to Nellis, Bill told me I had an option — sign in and stay at Nellis in the F-111 or take a change of assignment to F-4s at George AFB, San Bernadino, California. I asked Norm what he thought, and he said, "Take the F-4." Which is what I did. My deposit on the house was $50 and I lost $15 of it.

We said goodbye to our best friends, Bill and Wanda Delaplane, and headed off to George AFB. The F-4 Replacement Training Unit (RTU) was a six-month class for about 24 aircrews — front seaters (aircraft commanders) and back seaters (pilots or navigators — known as GIBs — Guy in Back). We were crewed with the same person for the entire class. My aircraft commander was Captain Bill Vasser. I was jealous of his sports car because he had an aircraft stick grip in place of the gear shift handle, and everything was hooked up to it — lights, radio, windshield wipers, turn signals, you name it.

Somehow, I was put in charge of videoing and synching the audio with the video for the class graduation (class clown) film. The stars of the film were Captain Johnny Jumper and Major Joe Basic. The same John Jumper became Chief-of-Staff of the Air Force. I'm sure he was proud when they showed portions of this class clown video at his retirement ceremony. I was only too happy to provide it!

In addition to the training, we had many special fun weekend activities such as scraping and rewaxing the floors, painting the walls, etc.

We lived in a triplex in Apple Valley, CA, in the middle of nowhere. We had a pet desert tortoise. To keep him from escaping when he was outside, I drilled a hole in the rear edge of his shell and put a ring in it to which we could attach a thin rope. When we moved, we let him go. The easiest of pets.

I remember one late afternoon we were standing outside watching a lightning storm. There was no rain, so we just admired the view. There was a Joshua tree about 100 feet away from the building. A lightning bolt struck the tree, and it erupted into flames. We were impressed, not to mention the newfound respect we had for lightning. I took a video of the "burning bush." The Bible got it right.

Close to where we lived was a seafood store. I struck up a conversation with the owner, Don Ferrarese. I recognized the name because he started his career with the Orioles in 1955 and played three years there before going to the Cleveland Indians, Chicago White Sox, Philadelphia Phillies, and St. Louis Cardinals. He told me about a semi-pro team he had and invited me to play. Woody Woodell, an Academy classmate and F-4 RTU classmate joined the team and played until RTU was over in June 1969. There were two more ex-major leaguers, a catcher and first baseman from the Yankees whose names escape me. I got to pitch and play shortstop. One day, we played at Stengel Field in Glendale, California. Casey was in the stands. This was the last time I played organized baseball until 2014.

At the graduation ceremony, I was very fortunate to win the top pilot award (GIBs) and top academic award. The class video was also a big hit. Several things were very unique. First, everyone in the class was in the video at the beginning with a split-second mug shot standing on the ramp. Second, aircraft do not back up. I experimented with the super 8 video camera and after trial and error realized that if I videoed an aircraft taxiing out with the camera held upside down, when spliced into the video backwards, the aircraft would appear to be backing into the parking spot. The audio was a challenge because it was on a tape that had to be timed so that when the video and audio were started together it would match up for half an hour. Third, we used the audio of Snoopy flying his Sopwith Camel against the Red Baron, when the F-4 was taking off and in flight. It was comical. I wish I could play it for you now.

From there, it was a blur of land survival at Fairchild AFB in Spokane, WA, water survival training at Homestead AFB, FL, and jungle survival at Clark AFB in the Philippines enroute to Ubon.

A few things stand out during land survival training. On our trek through the mountains, we made camp every evening by a stream. After setting up our shelters using one-half of a parachute canopy, we would take out our Meals Ready to Eat (MREs) by the fire. That is, all except me. I took my survival kit fishing line and hook, tied it to a stick, dug up a few worms, and caught around 5 minnow-sized fish each evening. By the time I got back to camp, everyone else had turned in for the night. I took the aluminum foil from the MREs that they had left by the coals, wrapped the entire fish in them including the head and guts, and laid them on the coals. I then had the most delicious meal. This ritual every night kept me from starving to death.

I am always puzzled when I watch "Survivor" on TV. One of the perks for winning a challenge is a nice meal. They either can't be starving, or they don't show the aftermath of eating all that food with everybody throwing up all over the place. When I had my first meal after a week of survival, I was full after about three bites, but it smelled and tasted so good I kept eating. A few minutes later, it was all gone. A newscaster who got a ride in an F-18 with the Blue Angels asked the pilot what he should eat before the flight. The pilot said bananas. The newscaster asked why. The pilot said because they taste the same way going down as they do coming back up.

The other thing that stands out is the POW camp training experience. I believe we spent three days and two nights in the simulated camp. At night, the air raid sirens would come on periodically and the lights would go out, simulating an enemy attack and camp blackout. I was the only one who escaped. I worked my way down a ditch during subsequent "blackouts," to an outhouse-sized wooden building to get a "chit" (like a poker chip) to show them I had escaped. I worked my way back to the camp and saw some of my comrades outside the camp in the field on a work detail. I snuck into the detail and stood up. As we went back into the camp, I showed the guard at the gate my chit. They were upset. Apparently, I wasn't supposed to sneak back into the camp. My reward was a piece of cake. I'll never forget it — the best cake I ever had, and I don't even remember what kind and don't care.

Water survival was just a few days, as I recall, but included dragging you in the water in a parachute harness behind a speedboat to see if you could roll over on your back and keep from drowning. Then they took you parasailing behind the boat, released you from the tow rope to make a water landing, and eventually, picked you up in a helicopter before the sharks got to you.

Jungle survival was just another adventure. They took us into the mountains on Luzon Island near Angeles City where the Negritos lived. That night we were to hide as best we could, and the Negritos would try to find us. If they did, we would give them a chit and they would get a bag of rice for every chit they turned in. We were told not to move after dark because the mountains were very treacherous with shear-cliffs dropping off 500 feet. I found a nice pile of brush and buried myself in the middle. I didn't move. You could see the Negritos moving around with flashlights. One found me. I gave him my chit. They found every one of us. We smelled different. It was no contest. If I had to do it again, I would eat their food for a week before hiding. The next morning, they extracted us by helicopter, lowering the "jungle penetrator" that we had to remember how to attach ourselves correctly so we wouldn't fall off to a sure death.

I arrived at Ubon in August 1969 and was assigned to the 497th Tactical Fighter Squadron (TFS) or "Night Owls." It was the only exclusive night squadron in Vietnam. The 497th was part of the famed 8th Tactical Fighter Wing (TFW) commanded previously by Col Robin Olds. The other three squadrons were the 433rd Satan's Angels, 435th, and 25th. Part of the Nite Owls mission was to provide cover for the AC-123 and AC-130 Spooky gunships, and to knock out any AAA (Anti-Aircraft Artillery) guns that fired on them. Around the November 1969 time frame, we started a Nite Owl FAC program. I ended up with 25 night-FAC missions before going to the Wolf FACs. One of the hairiest missions at night was delivering napalm at 500 feet above the ground in the karst mountains in Laos.

The Wolfs, as we were commonly called, consisted of six aircrews selected from the four squadrons (80 aircrews) at Ubon. With the bombing halt over North Vietnam, the Fast FAC mission was arguably the most dangerous mission at the time. Bob Gomez joined the unit several months after I did. The "normal" tour of duty was three months since it was so dangerous, and then you would return to your squadron. I don't know of anyone who did that because it was the most exciting flying in the world. We lost an average of one airplane a month and sometimes the crew as well. I spent six months there and flew 110 Wolf missions before my champagne (last combat) flight before heading home (total of 234 missions). It was a mixed blessing. You were glad you had survived the course, but you sure hated to leave this tight-knit group that you had flown with "forever." They were your family, and nothing bonds people closer together than combat, where your life literally depends on the people you are flying with.

During the time I was at Ubon, five pilots from the 497th were selected to fly with the Wolfs. When Neil Bynum, a back-seater, was lost, Fred Bieber took his place. Al Lucki and Bob Gomez were also Wolfs who were lost on the 23 Apr 70 mission. Fred made it to the end and when I left Ubon, that made 2 of 5 that survived.

The missions we flew were normally four hours. We would take off from Ubon and fly to the area and spend about 35 minutes on station, hit the KC-135 refueling tanker and fly another 35 minutes in the area, hit the tanker again and fly another 35 minutes. Fred Bieber was about my size, black hair and mustache, and we could be mistaken for one another. On one mission with Papa Wolf, Major Richard Pierson, he mistakenly thought he had flown the entire mission with Fred.

My Distinguished Flying Cross mission was with Heinz Cordes. We had found multiple 37-millimeter (mm) AAA guns to the west of Mu Gia Pass. We carried rocket pods on each wing with seven rockets in a pod. During the mission, we rolled in 14 times and fired all the rockets. Each time we rolled in, 37 mm tracers went by us on both sides. The F-4 strike fighters with a laser designator airplane and the others with 2000-pound bombs knocked out all the guns. It was a good day's work.

One thing different about combat flying is that there are no weekends or holidays. You are there to do a mission and want to be on the schedule every day. The most consecutive days that I flew in a row was 31. Typically, you would fly 15-20 days in a row and then get one off. When my day off came, I would try to find a flight with another group. I got three daytime FAC missions in an OV-10, and three night missions in AC-130 and AC-123 gunships.

Each pilot could take a week R&R (rest and recouperation or relaxation). I took mine to Sydney, Australia and attended a live concert by Peter, Paul, and Mary. This was in early 1970 and the famous Sydney Opera House was still under construction, being completed in 1973 after construction began in 1959.

We could also take three-day R&R's locally. They had a C-130 that would hop from base-to-base in Thailand, and you could get a ride with them. I met Lt Col Tom Kerkendall in Bangkok, and he was an aircraft commander of a C-130 that was an Airborne Command and Control Center (ABCCC) at night and was the controlling agency for all the Nite Owl missions coming out of Ubon. He invited me to Udorn Royal Thai Air Force Base to fly with him to see his side of the operation. So, I hopped on a C-130 to Udorn.

The first stop was at Nakhon Phanom (NKP) Royal Thai Air Force Base where we would spend the night before heading to Udorn the next morning. No sense wasting time at NKP, so I looked up my friend Jim George who was flying A-1E Skyraiders. He was about to go on a 4 ½ hour night Barrel Roll mission and I asked if I could tag along. He said sure. So, I got my life support equipment, and we headed out to the airplane. The F-4 was a relatively new airplane, with first deliveries in1963. The A-1 on the other hand debuted in 1945. As I walked up to the Skyraider, I could see grease and grime all over the airplane, and oil leaking out underneath onto the ramp. I thought, what the hell have I gotten myself into. I climbed in and we cranked up and taxied to the runway. I really felt like this was a throwback flight. The sound of the engine, versus the whine of a jet engine, was terrific. We took off and headed to the target area. No FAC, we just had a target to attack. We must have made 20 passes dropping everything but the kitchen sink.

When you roll in on the target in the F-4 from 5000 feet, trees are the size of toothpicks. When you roll in from 500 feet in an A-1, leaves are the size of your hand. Very exciting but somewhat nerve wracking to be up that close and personal for me.

On to Udorn the next morning. We briefed the mission and took off an hour or so before dark. We lost a generator and had to return to base to get a different C-130. Once on station the crew set up an orbit that they would fly for 10 hours or more. I went in the back where all the action was controlling the requests for fighters from the FACs and normal night missions. By two in the morning, I had seen everything I could comprehend in the back, so I ambled up to the cockpit. Tom put me in the copilot seat and the copilot went back to take a nap. I watched what Tom was doing to fly the orbits and where he was making the turns with the autopilot engaged. About three in the morning, I noticed that I was the only one awake in the cockpit. I was a Lieutenant. Tom was a Lieutenant Colonel. Do I wake him up or just fly the airplane myself? I decided on the latter. When we hit the northern turn point, I turned the dial, and the aircraft made a shallow bank and turned 180 degrees to the left. When we hit the southern turn point, I did the same thing. I made two complete orbits before

Tom woke up and resumed his normal duties. I never said a word to him — so mums the word. But I did write an article published in the Daedalus Flyer, entitled *How I Saved the War.* If I had not been awake, we may have flown into Chinese territory. When the dust settled, I had flown combat missions in six different aircraft, the F-4D, OV-10, A-1E, C-130, AC-130, and AC-123. I would add a seventh several years later in the A-7D.

I carried a Yashica super 8mm movie camera with me on most missions and got some great footage. When a new front seater joined the group, he was checked out be a front seater flying in the back and then turned over to an experienced back-seater (GIB) to fly several missions. I was up on the dusk patrol (last four hours of daylight) with a new front seater, or Fellow Up Front (FUF). I knew there were always guns (AAA) at the dog's head (a river that made the shape of a dog's head in one section) so we headed there and made a few practice rocket passes. The video shows the rocket leaving the airplane and 23mm AAA fire coming up at us on both sides — but not very accurate. We continued this for several minutes with similar results every time. We were rolling-in several thousand feet above the "normal" roll-in altitude just for safety's sake. I thought that as I was giving the FUF some practice at shooting rockets to mark a target under fire, the gunners on the ground were getting practice shooting at us. We know how to have a good time.

I could kick myself for not using the camera on another mission. We had just taken off out of Ubon to go into Steel Tiger when we were diverted to hook up with an F-4 Stormy FAC out of Da Nang heading to Ubon for an emergency landing. He had taken three 23-millimeter hits right between the engines. We joined up on his right wing and escorted him back to Ubon. On final, when they put the flaps down, the airplane started rolling to the left. We called for them to bailout. We saw both canopies leave the aircraft, books and anything loose in the cockpit come flying out, and both pilots ejected from the airplane. Both chutes opened, the airplane continued to roll inverted and impacted the ground in a huge fireball. They ejected about 500 feet above the ground. Both were rescued and celebrated their survival in the O'Club that night at Ubon. What a video that would have been. But I was too amped up to think of the camera, and a do-over was not an option.

Several missions stand out, but the most dangerous one happened on 4 March 1970. We were flying a mid-morning go to Mu Gia Pass, right on the Laos/North Vietnam border. This is one of the passes where the Ho Chi Minh trail goes through Laos into South Vietnam. Anyone familiar with Mu Gia knows there is a 3000-foot ridge to the west, a 5000-foot peak to the east, and the valley is 1500 feet. There were scattered to broken clouds from the surface to about 10,000 feet. My attention was drawn to the Radar Homing and Warning (RHAW) gear indicating enemy radar guns were painting us from across the border on the North Vietnam side. They would periodically fire a single large AAA round (85 or 105 mm) at us just for effect. You would see a large air burst. No serious threat. The threat that day was that the front seater had become disoriented in the clouds. When I looked at the instruments, we were in a 45-degree dive in the clouds, and I yelled pull up. Fortunately, the pilot had already started to pull. The altimeter bottomed out at 1800 feet. Knowing about altimeter lag in a steep dive, and the "floor" being 1500 feet, I don't know how we made it.

As we broke out of the clouds, I remembered a story about an elderly lady who was walking up the stairs in her home eating a piece of cake and passed away on the steps. She was miraculously brought back to life and one of the questions they asked her was about what she remembered. She replied that she had finished eating the cake. I thought that if I were dead maybe I'm dreaming that I am still flying. Solution — I'll pinch myself and if it hurts, I'm still alive. Good plan. Which is what I did. But way too aggressively. It hurt, thank heavens, but the bruise didn't go away for two weeks. I had a new lease on life — it wasn't my time — at the age of 24. Otherwise, it would have just been another case of no chutes, no beepers. I hope I have made the most of it.

Chapter 2
Baltimore, Maryland
(1945-1963)

I was born on 29 October, 1945 and grew up in Baltimore County, Maryland. My parents, Robert Jerome and Carlyn Muths, had three children — me, the oldest, my brother Ken, and my sister, Barb. We lived in a row house in Arbutus.

My dad's parents lived in a small cottage in Pennsylvania, a few hundred yards from Laurel Lake. My great aunt and uncle built the first log cabin at Laurel Lake. My grandfather and his younger brother Lester built just across the gravel road from them. It was a family area until others saw the wonders of this area. That was my Huckleberry Finn life. I would go up there every summer with Ken for two months, wearing nothing but swim trunks while we went fishing and frogging. And yes, we had a two-holer out back.

The only thing that I am a real expert at is frogging. It was illegal to catch them at night with a flashlight, so I caught them during the day with a fishing pole, gig, net, bare hands, and shot a fair amount. We must have eaten 500 frog legs over the eight summers we were there before I realized years later that they were a delicacy.

I started playing baseball when I was eight. At 14 they asked me to be a pitcher, and we won the championship that year. I was the best pitcher in the league and won the most valuable player award. Who knew!

My best friend, Gary Collison was my catcher. We had been together since first grade. His dad was the coach, and my dad was the assistant coach. We had been playing ball together in Little League since we were eight. After high school we went our separate ways, and it was 25 years later when we reconnected. He was living in the Atlanta area, and I was stationed in Fort Walton Beach, Florida. Not too far apart. I set up a reunion with his wife June so Gary would be surprised. I drove up to his home and rang the doorbell with my baseball glove on and, when he opened the door, threw the ball in the glove and said "Wanna play catch?" We have kept in contact ever since then.

When Gary's grandson, Ausen Hensel, expressed an interest in flying, "Grumpy" said I know just the guy. Austen, and his good friend Will Shuford, both seniors at University of Georgia, came up to Greeneville, Tennessee twice over several weeks, and both completed their solo with me on the same day. They are currently on scholarships from FLIGHT Foundation to complete their private pilot's license in Georgia.

I was good at sports and academics. My junior year of high school, my dad asked me, if I had a choice, would I prefer to go to West Point, Annapolis, or the Air Force Academy (AFA). I don't remember the event, but he said I thought for a minute and said AFA. The rest is history. All I ever wanted to do was play baseball. I never grew up dreaming of flying or being in the military.

I can only imagine that a guidance counselor at Woodlawn Senior High School was doing their job and contacted my folks suggesting that I might be a good candidate for a service academy. I really don't know to this day. But thank you if that is the case.

My parents lived on Allendale Road in Baltimore when I was born. We moved to Arbutus before I remembered anything. One thing I don't remember is a funny story. When I was 18 or 19, after a shower, I looked in the mirror at my backside, obviously for the first time, and noticed a large X across my whole bottom. Having no idea what that was all about, I called mom since I knew she would. Apparently, back when I was just learning to walk and was stumbling around the house naked (now I know where that little habit comes from) the houses had metal grates on the floor where the heat came out. I lost my balance and sat on the grate. I assume I screamed bloody murder and couldn't get off the grate. Mom rescued me but not before I had branded myself. It must have been severe, because the X didn't fade away until I was 23. Nice job, Mom. Funny how you think back to all those communal showers after gym class in school and no one said a thing. I can hear the cop now. "Ma'am is that your kid?" "Let me see his bottom. Yep — that's mine!"

My grandparents, Edgar (Dedad) and Florence (Nanny), taught me to love the outdoors — mountains, lakes, streams, you name it. I was told that I was the one who named all the grandparents and great-grandparents. Dedad and Nanny (Dad's mom and dad), Mamaw (Nanny's mother) and Meemaw (Mom's mother). The cabin was named in my honor — Tinker's knoll, The Powley's. They thought Tinker would be better than Stinker.

Dedad took me frogging from the time I was eight years old and my brother Ken and I fishing. Fishing was boring, at least the way we did it, in a boat on the lake with a worm waiting for something to bite. Maybe there just weren't any fish to catch. Ken is four years younger, but when he turned 8 or 9, he became my frogging partner, rowing the boat or paddling the canoe while I spotted 'em and caught 'em.

I'll never forget when I was around eight, I was in the middle of the canoe sitting in the bottom with Dedad in the front seat and Lester in the back. They were paddling along about 15 feet from the bank through some lily pads looking for frogs when, suddenly, Lester leaped out of the canoe into about two feet of water. He rushed to the shore, I saw something swimming away from the bank, and he stuck his hand under the water and grabbed a snapping turtle by the tail — a big one. If you know anything about snapping turtles, it's that they can reach halfway back to their tail and bite your fingers off. Well, I didn't know that at the time, but Lester just threw that thing into the canoe and got back in. All without rocking the canoe. He had obviously done this before, but without me along for the ride. Did I mention that I was sitting on the bottom of the canoe — not on a seat. Now I had company — a highly pissed-off giant snapping turtle. I wonder if he forgot that I was along, or just didn't like me or care. I don't remember the rest of the trip, probably because I was too frightened thinking where I was going to go if he came close. Probably out of the canoe. But I do have all my fingers and toes.

The family went to Laurel Lake almost every weekend of the year. I think my dad felt a certain sense of responsibility or obligation to his parents since he was now their only child. My dad's brother, Herbert Frank, was killed in a B-17 enroute to Europe during WWII. He was the aircraft commander at the age of 23. He was a star at Springfield College in Massachusetts — varsity soccer, ice hockey, and lacrosse. He had his own band as the drummer and played for many of the school dances. He volunteered for Aviation Cadets three months short of graduation. He had married Glenna three months before going overseas. Glenna eventually remarried and had a family, but never forgot Nanny and Dedad for the rest of their lives. Nan lived to be 98.

My mom's brother Bill died in his twenties of a disease I believe. Both of my parents essentially lived their adult lives as only children. I think I was named after both of their siblings — Herbert William.

We passed through a small town up and back to Laurel Lake called Gettysburg. From the time I can first remember going by the cannons and cannon balls stacked in pyramids along the road, I felt something special. I had no idea what happened there until a decade later, but I could feel that something special had happened there every time I saw it. It was indeed hallowed ground.

At the age of 12, Dedad took me small game hunting. He taught me to shoot at the age of eight — a Benjamin Air Rifle and single shot, break action .22, both of which I still have today. Since hunting was a winter activity and I was a student in Baltimore County, my parents took me to the bus station in downtown Baltimore on Friday after school. I rode the bus by myself to Gettysburg where Nan and Dedad would pick me up and drive the 25 miles to the cottage. I would hunt all day Saturday, go to church Sunday morning with them in Carlisle, and reverse the trip Sunday afternoon.

One weekend when I was 12 years old, the hunting around the cottage was poor so I decided to expand my area of operation. After a while, I realized nothing looked familiar. I was lost. I quickened my pace and eventually started running through the woods. Fortunately, I had read in some of the hunting and outdoor magazines that running through the woods was what you did when you were lost and panicked. I stopped running.

I sat down on a big rock and prayed as I had been taught to do in Sunday School. The thought came to me to look up. I did so and there was only one small opening in the tops of the trees, but through the opening I could see Pole Steeple, a small outcropping of rocks at the top of the mountain on the opposite side of Laurel Lake from our cottage. They were the only rock formation on the entire mountain ridge. Only problem was, they were 150 degrees in the "wrong" direction from the way I was running. My 12-year-old brain had a hard time doing the math. So, I got up and kept on going the same way I had been running. After a hundred feet or so, I stopped. Now reason set in. I thought that if I had prayed and received an answer to that prayer, I should follow it. So, I took off heading to Pole Steeple. About 45 minutes later I could see the boy scout camp that was about half a mile behind our cottage. I was elated. It was getting dark, and I was out longer than I had ever been. As I came onto the back lawn from the woods, Nan was there waiting for me. We gave each other a big hug and went inside. No one spoke a word. I'm sure she had also been praying and knew what had just happened. I was home safe and sound. This is when I learned the power of prayer that would stay with me for the rest of my life. Thank you, Father!

My grandparents sold the cottage when I was 16 due to my grandfather's illness and moved to Towson, Maryland to live with Nan's sister. He passed a short time later. My world was turned upside down. My idyllic childhood was over, my grandfather and all the guy things we did together were gone, but Laurel Lake will always have a special place in my heart.

My brother and I have recreated the adventures there over the past six decades. On one adventure frogging on Laurel Lake, we met two gentlemen from Gettysburg who were fishing. We found out they had many ponds, and they invited us up to catch some frogs.

Ken and I took them up on their offer. Our idea was to catch them with a light at night and restock Laurel Lake, whose frog population was way down. The first time we went there, we scouted the ponds and channels in the daytime to get a lay of the land. There were many fences with electric wires on them. We were going to use one of Ken's eight-man rafts from his Whitewater Challengers river-rafting company.

As nighttime approached, we geared up. Ken would guide the raft from the rear, and I would sit in the front with a headlamp and catch the frogs, who were blinded by the light, with my hands. We would put them in a large ice chest and transport them to Laurel Lake and release them.

Our first stop was a small pond only 50 feet from their house in the back yard. We got 36 frogs from that little pond. They were everywhere. We were excited. The other ponds were across the road and required us to portage the raft for a distance. This was a good-sized raft.

We put the raft in one area that was flooded by beaver dams. We had to open a metal gate to get out of the fenced in area to the channel and other ponds. We got out of the raft on the other side of the channel and lugged it several hundred feet to another shallow pond. After several hours we decided to call it quits. Coming back to the channel with the raft, I took one step too far, and found myself up to my neck in water. I could see my watch glowing under the water. I managed to climb out and we got in the raft to go to the other side.

Now we had to get to the van, which required us to throw the raft uphill over the fence and wiggle under the electric part of the fence. Did I mention that I was soaking wet? We made several attempts to throw the raft over the fence and finally got it. Then, Ken and I managed to get under the fence without electrocuting ourselves.

It was about three in the morning, and I had to change clothes. The side doors of the van were just a few feet from the road, so I had to strip down naked (there I go again) and change clothes right by the road. Fortunately, there was no traffic on this little road at that time in the morning. We drove an hour to Laurel Lake and released about 80 frogs. I am just blessed to know how to have a good time. Ken said it was like Vietnam without the bullets.

We held Nan's 90th birthday party at Laurel Lake in a rental cabin. We thought it would be nice to see the cottage with Nan if anybody was there. The kids of the couple that had purchased the cabin were there. They invited us in. Well, you could have knocked us over with a feather. This was 25 years after they bought the cabin. Absolutely nothing was changed. Talk about déjà vu. We couldn't believe it, and still can't to this day. Nothing had changed. Our family pictures were still hanging on the wall.

I went out on the screened-in porch to Dedad's office. When I looked through the drawers of his desk, everything was still there from the last time he sat there. I took a 1955 Reader's Digest subscription letter and an old pen knife of his. There was a photo of my Uncle Herbert when he was a small boy of about two or three petting the family dog. The frame was an old rounded top with slightly rounded glass covering the picture. The kids called their parents to see if it would be ok for us to take it. They said sure. It is now hanging in the guest bedroom of our home. I wish we could have taken everything that was there. I would have my ashes spread there should I ever die.

I never questioned why I was called Bill. It just seemed natural since I've always gone by that name. When I was 50, Nan asked me if I knew why I went by Bill. I said no. She said Dedad had a brother Herbert who was killed in WW I, his son Herbert, of course, was killed in WW II, and the name Herbert was just too painful to hear. So, I was called Bill. I'm glad I wasn't called Herbert in Vietnam.

Chapter 3
Colorado Springs, Colorado
(1963-1967)

My first airplane ride was with my parents going to Colorado Springs, Colorado in June 1963 to join the then Thin Blue Line at the United States Air Force Academy (USAFA). The first graduating class was in 1959 who began their careers at Lowry Air Force Base in Denver. They moved to the Academy in 1958. I arrived just 6 years after it opened.

I won't go into great detail about the Academy experience. Suffice it to say if you have attended one you know what it is, if you haven't, you never will. There was a lot of yelling and screaming and lines to form, shots to be had, hair to be cut, running and push-ups to be done. Basic summer was a blur but as a musician in high school, playing French horn in the band and trumpet in the dance band, I despised the Academy band. Every morning, you would wake up to them marching down the terrazzo along the dorms in Vandenberg Hall and you knew — you sure as hell knew — that nothing good was going to happen for the rest of the day. And you were right. More banging on doors, yelling and screaming, getting dressed in 10 seconds, running to formation, more yelling and screaming, rack it back smack, marching to all the meals, answering cadet knowledge questions, thousands of push-ups, eating at attention for the rest of your life, or so it seemed. A fun time was had by all — well, maybe by the upperclassmen.

After summer basic training, recognition day finally arrived. This meant we had met the basic military requirements — the bad news is we got to stay at the Academy — more of the same for another year with academics thrown in just for grins. Hurray!

One thing I knew is that I did not want to sit at the squadron tables for meals. I tried out for the freshman soccer team since I played varsity soccer in high school. I was the last cadet cut from the team. First time I had ever been cut from anything in my life. Well, this officially sucks. I looked at the list a dozen times and could not make my name appear on the roster. Now what? I decided I was a gymnast and joined the freshmen gymnastics team. I had never done gymnastics in my life. So now I was not eating as much as before to lose the weight I had gained at the soccer tables (one reason I was probably cut from the team because I wasn't as fast as I should have been) and doing hand-stand push-ups in my room at night. I was on the pommel horse — only because no one else wanted to do it. You ever try that — don't. As I said, I had no previous experience, but the Academy didn't have world class gymnasts at that point. I do have to admit that I probably own, or at least share an NCAA record for the least number of points for a Division I competitive routine — ½ point. That was a gift. I don't think they do quarter points.

I did play varsity soccer my junior year. I used my Uncle Herbert's lacrosse sticks to play two years of intramural lacrosse for 3rd Squadron. USAFA is the number one (or close to it) jock school in the country. Everyone plays sports. We went to the wing championship both years. My junior year we won, my senior year we lost. I was the leading scorer on the team both years. I had never played lacrosse before in my life, but I was from Baltimore and had professional sticks so everybody thought I could. Go figure.

My real claim to fame was being the captain of the skeet team. A new first for the Academy. What a treat to be able to go to the range and shoot skeet several times a week for free. Free is good. After graduation, I only continued shooting for about a year as a Lieutenant because it cost too much — and I was busy. The skeet team consisted of five cadets and set two Collegiate World Skeet Records — 1966 for 1000 targets, and 1967 for 500 targets. Nobody at the Academy then or now knows about this except the skeet team.

I felt like I was in way over my head and had to work every weekend for four years to either catch up or get a little ahead. I went to church every Sunday morning in Colorado Springs and spent the afternoon with retired naval Captain Charlie Bond and his wife, Kay. For four years this ritual was a saving grace and gave me some space and calm to cope with the rigors of Academy life. Charlie Bond commanded a supply carrier during WW II and accompanied Admiral Byrd on one expedition to the South pole. He was a terrific gentleman, and I owe him and Kay all the thanks in the world.

My hard work earned me spots on the Dean's list, Commandant's list and Superintendent's list, but rarely at the same time. Most of the time this inconsistency caused me to keep changing the insignia on my uniform sleeve, which, unfortunately, required removing the old one and sewing on the new one.

I met some terrific cadets and future warriors and leaders in my four years. The first semester of my senior year, I roomed with Ted Legasy. He was the Group Commander. I was the Group Operations Officer. He is a Distinguished Graduate. That is high, high cotton.

My second semester roommate was Bob Grow. We had a brilliant plan to take a hiking and fishing trip up in the high country before graduation. We packed our tent and fishing gear in the trunk of his new Bonneville Pontiac. We drove up into the mountains as far as the road would go (paved, then gravel, then dirt). We hiked to a small stream and set up camp. We spent the night and next morning set out to fish in the small lakes. We put our drinks in the stream to keep them cool.

One minor flaw in our plan. We should have packed ice skates. This was the last week of May, but the lakes were frozen solid. Well, it was a great hike and beautiful scenery around the timber line. The evening meal of hot dogs and Pepsi by the fire was like filet mignon after a long day on the trail. There was a light snow that night which made breaking camp and hiking out another adventure.

Graduation day is special. I have been back about five times to see my high school cadets graduate. The march-on still brings tears to my eyes. It is spectacular. Doing it yourself is surreal. It's hard to believe it is over. The day after graduation, I got married in the cadet chapel to my high school sweetheart, Linda Roberts. Both immediate families attended. My brother Ken was my best man. Eight classmates were saber bearers. To this day, the Academy experience is the toughest thing I have ever done. I think it's designed that way. It makes everything else you do seem easy — or maybe just because it's fun. Pilot training, combat flying, whatever, I would do again before I would go back through those four years at USAFA. But I am proud to have done it, graduating at the bottom of the top third. And it's a great place to visit.

Chapter 4
Lubbock, Texas
(1967-1968)

Following graduation and marriage, Linda and I set out on our honeymoon. I'm not sure she voted for this, but she was a good sport. We set out on a 10,000-mile camping/cross country trip.

We left Colorado Springs and headed north for Banff and Lake Louise in Alberta, Canada. We camped along the way at Rocky Mountain National Park, Grand Teton National Park, Yellowstone National Park, and Glacier National Park. It was magical to see the snow in June, beautiful scenery, and wildlife. Banff and Lake Louise were exquisite, and I remember the hike up to the Tea House in the snow where chipmunks would sit on your hand and eat peanuts.

From Banff we headed east to Liberty, Saskatchewan, where we met my roommate Bob Grow to do some fishing. We caught a lot of Walleye by trolling and had some great eating. I did mention that this was our honeymoon, right?

From there we worked our way to Chicago and then to Baltimore where we had a reception for all the family and friends who couldn't make it to Colorado for the wedding. Then we headed for my first duty assignment at Reese AFB in Lubbock, Texas for pilot training.

When we came through Wichita Falls, Texas, it was 114 degrees. That was hot compared to Colorado Springs. We arrived in Lubbock,

Texas in early August, having used my 60 days free leave and travelling 10,000 miles to end up less than 500 miles from USAFA.

I was on my own now, married, excited, but apparently not ready to resume the rigors of study, which I had just escaped. After completing T-41 (the military version of the Cessna-172) training, designed as a cheap way to weed out those students who really couldn't fly, we started into jet training in the T-37. I bombed our first test, T-37 operations. We had 85 students in our class, and I was now flunking out and ranked 84 out of 85. Shit! Not the way I wanted to start my Air Force career. That was my wake-up call. I aced the next two exams, and ended up 14th in academics, 5th in flying, and 9th overall. We graduated 55 pilots.

Bill Delaplane, his wife Wanda, Linda and I got together for dinner as often as we could. None of us will forget one evening at the Delaplane's. Wanda made pumpkin spice ice cream in a champagne glass that had been in the freezer. She served it and I immediately took it, sitting it down on the table. The base must have hit at an angle because I was left holding only the stem with the top rolling around on the table. It only took about two years to replace the set. Fortunately, our friendship survived.

Linda and I became parents about 9 months after we got to Lubbock — a fate that befell a lot of couples released from prison. Being new to this thing, we didn't know what was going on in the beginning. Everyone else did. We were in church one Sunday morning and just as the service ended Linda leaned over and ralphed all down the front of my sports jacket. I thought that was rude of her, but we finally figured it out and all was forgiven.

Our best friends from church, Jack and Delorus (Auntie Duck) Norred befriended us early on and we spent many days at their house playing Yahtzee. Their son, Kenny, became my hunting buddy and we spent many weekends and evenings hunting quail, rabbits, and sandhill cranes.

I took up taxidermy and Jack, a retired Air Force Master Sergeant, let me use his place to keep wooden barrels full of brine to tan deer skins, which I got from a company processing deer meat for local hunters. Most of my taxidermy involved preserving quail and pheasant skins, which I still have today, and doing simple things like mounting heads of game birds on a plaque.

My hunting prowess and that of many others were put on display that year. One of the dangers of flying at Lubbock was the sandhill cranes. They are huge birds and can do serious damage to a T-38, like knocking it out of the sky. Lubbock was on their migratory path south and north. Several avid hunters, including my classmate Dale Stoval, now a retired Brigadier General and recipient of the Air Force Cross, for his heroic rescue of Roger Locker in a Jolly Green helicopter in North Vietnam, took the Wing Commander, Col Clyde Morganti, hunting sandhill cranes and groveling around in the mud several times.

The other hazard at the base was jack rabbits running all over the place including the runways. Nothing seemed to discourage them. Finally, with all non-lethal options exhausted, we had a redneck option that worked. We got several pick-up trucks, loaded them up with hopefully sober pilots in the truck bed with shotguns (what could possibly go wrong with this scenario) and ran the trucks up and down the entire length of the runway and taxiway and all grassy points in between and took out a bunch of jack rabbits.

Following graduation, I had the opportunity to spend a week with Dale at his home in Toppenish, Washington, do some duck, pheasant, and quail hunting, and see how revered he was by his high school community. It remains a highlight of my early days in the Air Force.

Our son Robert Carl (Bobby) arrived in April of '68 and a new chapter of our lives was born. Being the first grandchild in either family came with a lot of responsibility for him, but he didn't seem to care too much. At least we didn't have any floor grates in our apartment in Lubbock.

All-in-all, it was a most enjoyable and instructive year, filled with new friends and adventures. Sadly, they remain as memories, because we never saw the Norreds again, and Bill Delaplane would not live to see his 30th birthday.

Chapter 5
Myrtle Beach, South Carolina
(1971-1974)

Following my tour of duty in Vietnam, I came back to the states and stayed with Bill and Wanda in Las Vegas, Nevada. Linda met me there from Baltimore where she had spent my time at Ubon with my parents. When we met, I saw my second son Kenneth William (Billy) for the first time. He was born in March 1970, and was now three months old. I had not seen Linda or Bobby for 10 months. The Delaplanes were kind enough to keep the kids so Linda and I could get reacquainted in a hotel in Las Vegas.

From Las Vegas we headed to my next assignment at Homestead AFB, Florida. We lived on base housing for the first and only time. I went TDY (Temporary Duty) to MacDill AFB in Tampa, FL for two months to upgrade to the front seat of the F-4.

One of the special missions at Homestead was hurricane evacuation. It was our duty to save the airplanes and fly them to Tinker AFB in Oklahoma and play golf or tennis while our families stayed at Homestead to weather the hurricane. We did this twice in the little time I was there. Coming back to Homestead, the pine forests on the base looked like a war zone. It seemed like half the trees were down. When cleaned up and time passed the woods still seemed full of trees. The families fared well, which is great because I would have felt even worse about leaving them than I already did.

One mission stands out to me. Back in the day, they had firepower demonstrations for the local civilian population. The base would set up bleachers a reasonable distance from the range and we would drop bombs, shoot rockets, and fire the 20mm cannons. It was a good show. This mission, we were a single ship F-4 intercepting two F-100s right in front of the stands. Our speed for the entry was supersonic at 100 feet (670 Knots or 770 miles per hour). That's fast folks. You see ridge lines flashing by. Picture NASCAR at 800 miles an hour. The sense of speed is relative to how close you are to the ground. At Mach 2 at 30,000 feet, the only thing that moves is the fuel gauge. But this was hauling ass. I have never seen anything like it before or after.

Soon after upgrading, I was fortunate to get an assignment to Myrtle Beach AFB, South Carolina to the first A-7D squadron in the Air Force, the 353rd TFS in the 354th TFW (Tactical Fighter Wing).

Housing was scarce so we took the plunge and bought our first home. I remember vividly the trepidation we had trying to convince ourselves we could afford it. We cancelled all our magazine subscriptions (which weren't many) and thought of anything else we could live without, to lower our payments. We used our first VA (Veterans Administration) loan. It would prove to be a good move in the long run.

To get checked out in the A-7 we had to go to Davis-Monthan AFB in Tucson, Arizona. Another adventure, driving two cars, a station wagon and MGB with two kids and enough stuff to last us for three months. We rented a small house in the middle of a trailer park. It was dusty and required a lot of work. I think it used to be the trailer park manager's house. Fortunately, we were only there a short time.

A-7 training was exciting. We trained in Navy A-7s with the probe on the side instead of the single point refueling receptacle behind the pilot on top of the fuselage. This had the advantage that you could give someone the finger when you taxied by extending the probe. There were no simulators or two-seaters. Ground school was thus intense and very important. The first flight consisted of a supervised start (instructor standing on the side of the cockpit to observe) and then he went to his own airplane. Another first and confidence builder. Your first flight, and everyone thereafter, was solo. Single seat, single engine, baby!

Back at Myrtle Beach, we started the moving-in process, buying furniture for our first home, and getting acquainted with my new squadron mates. I had enough rank as Captain that I was not automatically the snack bar officer. Half of the squadron were new lieutenants right out of pilot training. This was the only squadron that I have been in that had the perfect rank structure. Most squadrons are top heavy with Majors and Lieutenant Colonels. We had a Lt Col for a commander, Major for an Ops Officer, and Captains and Majors as Flight commanders. Most two ship formations were a Major or Captain Element leader and Lieutenant as wingman. And these lieutenants were good.

The most harrowing thing that happened at Myrtle Beach happened one evening in our home. Linda was going out for the evening, and I got to take care of the kids. You see the problem right away. No sweat, I told her. I got this. Have a great time. The boys were in a bunk bed with Bobby, the oldest, on top and Billy underneath.

Time for me to watch TV. All quiet on the western front, until I heard a horrendous crash. I rushed into the bedroom and saw that Bobby had fallen out of the top bunk onto the floor. I thought I had killed him. I'm not sure what it means when you look like you're screaming but no sound is coming out. Not good I'm sure of that. I hugged him and walked him into the living room. Finally, he made a noise — progress. Oh my God. What have I done? Don't remember how long he cried or when he went back to bed after I built a bomb shelter around the top bunk, but he eventually went back to sleep. Linda came home. How did it go? Great. Any problems? Nope. I was safe and off the hook if Bobby didn't wake up the next morning with a tennis ball size knot on his head. Then I'd have some 'splaining to do.

The next great new adventure was the deployment of the 354th TFW to Korat in October 1972. The 353rd (big red machine) was the last squadron to depart Myrtle on 12 October. We had the families at the base, on the ramp, waving good-bye as we taxied to the runway. We flew from Myrtle to Davis-Monthan (4.1 hours), to Hickam (6.8 hours), to Guam (7.5 hours), to Korat (6.5 hours). That's a lot of time sitting in a small cockpit where you can't move around. We were tired. Along the way we picked up a few stragglers from the other squadrons who had maintenance issues. When we landed at Korat on 16 October, the entire wing was there.

We began flying missions a few days later. We were welcomed by the F-105 Thud drivers because we had a longer takeoff roll than they did. Taking off with twelve 500-pound bombs with no afterburner took a lot of runway. Once airborne, the airplane handled like a dream and could stay on station for one and a half hours verses 30 minutes for the F-4. With the head-up display and computer bombing system, accuracy was unreal.

One mission proves this point. I was number two in a three ship. Lead had CBU's (Cluster Bomb Units) and 2 and 3 had 500-pound bombs. The FAC had two huge Quonset-hut style buildings he wanted destroyed. He wanted us to drop single bombs. Lead had no ordnance to release on this target. As number two, I would be the first one to strike the target. Since the FAC had never worked A-7s before, I asked if I could drop two bombs. He said sure. I estimated the distance between the two structures as 50 meters, put that distance in the computer, and selected two bombs to be released with the appropriate interval between them. I rolled in, put the pipper, the aiming reticle on the head-up display (HUD), right in the middle between the two huts, hit the pickle (bomb release) button with my thumb on the stick grip, and pulled off on the bomb fall line. The bombs released, I rolled over and looked down and saw both huts disappear. The FAC said that's all I got, so we had to rendezvous with another FAC on a new target. That's what the A-7 could do.

In mid-December, we were headed to the hootches from the flight line when we noticed they were loading AIM-9 Sidewinder heat seeking missiles on our A-7s. The A-7 held one on each side of the fuselage. What's going on, we wondered. That night we found out. We had a meeting in our commander's room — we were going "downtown."

This was the start of Linebacker II. The ops officer, now a Lt Col, briefed and led the mission. Throughout the briefing, the commander, a veteran of 100 F-105 missions over North Vietnam, including "downtown" Hanoi, kept muttering "that's a bad place."

The briefing the next morning was at 0400. Over the next two weeks, we pounded Hanoi day and night. Sadly, the B-52s took the brunt of the enemy defenses. Every day we went to the morning brief and looked at the SAR (Search and Rescue) board and we would see several B-52s had been shot down the night before. The A-7s had taken over the A-1 Sandy (search and rescue) role. We were busy with SAR missions and bombing missions every day.

One mission stands out. The mission was four 4-ships (16 airplanes). The weather was bad and after aerial refueling, we had to join up on an F-111 Aardvark to sky spot. He would lead us to the target and give us all the command to drop the bombs. The formation looked like a WW II Ploesti raid. We had 8 A-7s on his left wing and 8 on his right wing, all line abreast.

It was comical to hear Red Crown directing the F-4 Mig Cap aircraft against the Migs. They would call Migs at 12 o'clock low 10 miles, 12 o'clock low 5 miles, 6 0'clock low 2 miles, then, they would turn the F-4s 180 degrees and repeat the same calls. You could visualize them going back and forth in between the cloud decks but not wanting to engage.

After we dropped our bombs, the F-111 lit the burners, said adios, and egressed at about 700 knots. We formed up in our four 4-ship formations. We were doing 450 knots at 15,000 feet. It was basically a cross-country flight over Hanoi with Migs present. During the morning briefing, when we were assigned the fourth (rear) flight position Harry Johnson, the flight lead looked at me and we mouthed "cannon fodder" to each other. The good news for us was that the Migs were no threat due to weather, and the enemy defenses were being conserved for the nighttime B-52 strikes. The other good news was that Linebacker II insured diplomatic negotiations resulted in the release of 591 POWs starting in February 1973.

Since we were there TDY, the squadron pilots returned to Myrtle Beach the end of January 1973. Somewhere during my flying at Myrtle, I had another first. Before I get to that, I have to give you the first and only tutorial. Four fighters flying in close formation, similar to what the Air Force Thunderbirds, or Navy Blue Angels fly in their airshows, is called "fingertip formation." Take your left hand and fold your thumb underneath your fingers. When you look at the top of your hand you see the fingertip formation. The middle finger is lead (number 1), the index finger is lead's wingman (number 2), the ring finger is the element leader (number 3), and the pinkie finger is the element leader's wingman (number 4). In this case the second element (numbers 3 and 4) are on the leader's left. Do the same thing with your right hand and you will see that the second element is on the leader's right. This is the formation we were flying on our way back to Myrtle Beach from the bombing range. Harry Johnson was the leader, Jack Welde was number two, Jay Reidel was number 3 and yours truly was "blue 4".

We were around 15,000 feet and there were white puffy clouds throughout the area. No rain, not bumpy, just towering cumulus clouds. We entered the clouds under Air Traffic Control (ATC) vectors to Myrtle Beach. I tucked in closer to three and eventually all I could see was the wingtip light. Then I wouldn't see it. Then I would. After this went on for a little while, eventually I couldn't see it for several seconds.

There is a procedure for this called lost wingman. When you must go lost wingman, which I did, I called "four's out" and turned away from the formation 30 degrees for 30 seconds and then turned back to the original heading. This presumes that you are straight and level (not in a banked turn) to begin with. The transition from staring at the wing tip light to moving your head to the instrument panel to find out what attitude you are in and making a 30-degree bank turn is very disorienting. I had never known anyone who had gone lost wingman. It kind of has the implication that you can't hack it. I felt bad until three seconds later when I heard, threes out, twos out. I didn't feel so bad anymore.

When we broke out of the clouds, we were in a very wide route formation. Take your fingers and spread them as far apart as you can.

This is route formation, which allows you to look around and be more relaxed than fingertip formation. Harry rocked his wings which is the signal to return to fingertip formation. We all got back in, me being the last of course, just seconds before we went into the next set of clouds. Same result. Fours out, threes out, twos out. At least now, I had some recently gained experience at this thing. After we broke out of the clouds the second time, Harry thought we had enough practice so he told ATC we would be recovering single ship. Not too many pilots have ever had to go lost wingman, but I am sure we are the only ones who did a four-ship lost wingman procedure twice in three minutes.

We returned to Korat in April. It was during this second TDY that I had my second close call. The golden BB missed me again.

We were on a bombing mission and were taking fire from some 37mm batteries. The FAC marked them with a 2.75 white phosphorus rocket and I rolled in. On my first pass, a 37mm tracer the size of a tennis ball went right over my head less than an inch from the canopy. I could have reached up and grabbed it without extending my whole arm. Scared the crap out of me. I jumped in my seat and the bomb went somewhere.

Rolling in on AAA guns is dangerous because you solve their lead pursuit aiming problem. Since the tail of the A-7 is higher than the canopy, I can't explain how it missed the tail. The gunner had me dead to rights. Knowing also they shoot in clips of 5 shells, he had me wired. I can only presume that I was in the V with one round that I did not see just under me. Two seconds after the scare, things were back to normal. We silenced the guns.

After two combat tours, I realized that the closer you are to death (when you are young and healthy that is) the more you feel alive. It explains why so many people do so many crazy things.

On 15 August 1973, the air war stopped because the funding had been cut off. One day we were flying combat, the next day we were dropping 25-pound BDU-33s on a practice range in Thailand. I ended up with 347 combat missions and 1000 combat hours in 20 months in the F-4 and A-7, one-third of my 3000 hours accumulated over15 years of flying in the Air Force.

Morale was at an all-time low. I decided to organize a slow-pitch softball tournament for the entire Wing. It lasted about two months. The championship game was announced just like a world series game. The Wing Commander threw out the first pitch. Our squadron (353rd) won the championship and the event was mentioned in my Meritorious Service Medal presentation.

The squadron pilots were back in Myrtle Beach in October 1973 and transitioned to a combat crew training squadron.

Chapter 6
Bill Delaplane
(1973-1974)

As soon as we returned to Myrtle Beach, I was checked out as a flight instructor and had my first student. Flying your own airplane is fun — you get as much stick time as your student. But it gets complicated when things go awry. One night flight we were holding at 15,000 feet to make an instrument approach to Myrtle Beach. The weather was crap, and I started to pick up ice on the wind screen. Eventually, I had to take charge of the flight, make all the radio changes and calls, get us to a lower altitude, all while flying on the wing in weather. Makes flight instruction in the same plane seem simple.

On 21 December 1973, around 9 pm, the phone rang at our house. Linda answered it and said it was for me. It was the Cannon AFB Command Post notifying me that Bill Delaplane had just been killed in an F-111 crash. It was a night, terrain following mission, and they had struck the ground. Both crew members were killed.

Again, like Bob Gomez, I have an indelible picture of the room. The dining table with a traffic light type lamp hanging overhead, glowing red, Paul Rossetti seated at the left end and Linda at the right end. Our Air Force family was once again suffering and in need. Wanda's first call was to me. The next several weeks would be very emotional. Wanda requested that I be her escort officer which I accepted without hesitation.

This was a terrible loss to the Delaplane family, his third squadron classmates at the Air force Academy, and the Air Force. "Kerlin" came to the Academy after a year of college and was a standout in every sense of the word. His senior year he was the squadron commander for one semester. Only two seniors in each squadron get to be the commander. They don't just give those away. I am convinced that he would have been a general had this tragedy not occurred.

Bill and Wanda were high school sweethearts. Wanda was a cheerleader and Bill was the captain of the basketball team. Go figure! They graduated from high school together and Bill went off to Eastern Illinois University in Charleston, Illinois for a year before attending the Air Force Academy. Bill and Wanda were married about a month and a half after graduation on 22 July 1967 in Mansfield, Illinois. The reception was held at Bill's parent's house in the back yard, and it was very hot. In August of 1970, Bill and Wanda adopted a five-day old baby boy they named Billy while stationed at Nellis AFB in Las Vegas, Nevada.

Bill had a Vietnam tour as a forward air controller (FAC) in the O-2 stationed in Saigon, South Vietnam from September 1971 to October 1972. Following his return stateside they were re-assigned to Cannon AFB, New Mexico.

Linda and I drove to Mansfield, Illinois where the funeral would take place. As Wanda's escort, I would be with her all day making sure she was OK and had everything she needed. Another officer was making the funeral arrangements. The day of the funeral I was the one who presented the folded American flag from his coffin to Wanda. All I could say was "Auntie Wanda, on behalf of a grateful nation…" I was afraid I was going to lose it.

After the funeral and all arrangements were completed, Linda and I drove home. I remember telling Linda that it was so emotional that I felt like I wanted to marry Wanda. I am thankful that I have not been called upon to do that again.

I have kept in contact over the years and am grateful to call her a wonderful friend. She went to law school on the GI bill and was very grateful because she would not have been able to afford it otherwise. She graduated from the University of Kentucky in May 1984. Most of her career was spent in the office of the Attorney General of Kentucky working in consumer protection. When in court, she was addressed as madame attorney general, or general Delaplane. The first time she heard that, her jaw dropped. She has been a big fan of FLIGHT Foundation and has sponsored female students to solo in honor of Bill's mom.

Chapter 7
Eglin AFB, Florida
(1974-1977)

(A Career Ending Day)

After my first student at Myrtle Beach, I was sent to Squadron Officer's School at Maxwell AFB, Montgomery, Alabama. I was disappointed that I did not make distinguished graduate, but I did make top third. Returning to Myrtle Beach, I received a plumb assignment in July 1974. I was going to Eglin AFB in Fort Walton Beach, Florida to the 3246th Test Wing as the only Tactical Air Command (TAC) pilot in the predominantly Test Pilot School Graduates community. I would be doing munitions test flights with them in the A-7 and dual current in the T-38.

We sold the house in Myrtle Beach and bought our first brand new house in a new development in Shalimar, Florida. The kids were in school, Linda was managing the family as usual, and Happy Ann and her pup Heidi were roaming the house.

One of my test missions was the Piranha mine. To test the deployment of the mine from the cannister loaded on one of the pylons on the airplane, two test runs were made on a rectangle about 100 feet long and 50 feet wide filled with water. The run-in was level at 400 knots about 200 feet AGL (Above Ground Level). The test engineers had it all calculated to give me the command to pickle (release the mines). The first run I followed their command, and all the mines hit short of the water. We had one more chance. As we set up for the second run, they said they were going to recalculate it. I didn't trust their calculations since they missed it the first time. I said give me the same release point and I'll make the adjustment. My Kentucky windage told me a one second delay from their release point would work. They said "pickle", I said, "a thousand one" and hit the button. What a great WAG-Wild Ass Guess! Every mine splashed in the water. I have the pictures to prove it.

The worst day of my Air Force career occurred on the range when I was doing a low level 50-foot AGL bomb run. It was late afternoon, and the sun was in my eyes, so I decided to come in 90 degrees from the normal run-in line, it took me straight into a tree line. I knew better, but calculated when I should pull up to miss the trees. Everything was fine until I got a call that evening at home that they were picking pine needles out of my wing tip. The left-wing tip light was broken. It cost $26 to fix it, but my career, as it was, was over. I was grounded for 30 days, had to write a manual on bombing range procedures, and flying was never the same.

This incident happened to coincide with the new OER (Officer Effectiveness Report) 1-2-3 system. Three put you in the bottom 50 percent of your contemporaries. I got two of them in succession. The result was I got passed over to major the first time and to Lt Col the first time. I only got promoted the second time around to each rank because the Generals I was working for went to bat for me. One thing in my favor is that I never quit working. I truly loved flying and the Air Force. So, I stayed in.

One thing that kept me going was our church family. I was a Sunday School teacher, and we were adopted by many of the local church members. One couple had property in DeFuniak Springs with several small lakes. My best investment, to this day, was a 10-foot john boat for $67. I still have it. We traded our Buick Skylark which I had purchased at the Air Force Academy for $3000 for a Chevy station wagon. Like a million other young couples with growing families. The boat slid perfectly in the back. Bobby, Billy, and I spent at least three weekends a month fishing on the Pendery's lakes every Saturday. That has led to a lifelong fishing adventure. I will always be grateful to the Pendery's, Lester's, and the rest of our church family in Fort Walton Beach.

Chapter 8
Fort Worth, Texas
(1977-1981)

My next assignment was to the new F-16 program in Fort Worth, Texas at the General Dynamics production facility which shared the runway with Carswell AFB. I would be flying new airplanes off the production line - Acceptance Test Procedures (ATP) - to guarantee they met contract specifications before they were delivered to the Air Force.

We sold the house in Shalimar and moved into a bigger, brand-new house in south Fort Worth. We were working our way up to the east side. Happy Ann had passed in Shalimar and Heide, a Beagapoo, was our only pet.

The fishing tradition continued, at least three Saturdays a month, mostly on Benbrook Lake, about 20 minutes from our house on Brandingshire Place. The weather never bothered us — at least not the cold. One day in December we were trolling by the dam, freezing out butts off with fur coats, caps, and mittens on. I noticed that Billy was not fishing. When I inquired, I discovered that he had cast his lure, rod, and reel at the fish. The rod had slipped out of his hand since they were frozen. We spent about 30 minutes throwing deep divers along the dam to see if we could snag his line. No luck. We called it a day.

We met a new church family, where I was again a Sunday School teacher and later Sunday School Superintendent.

The F-16 is a terrific airplane, as history has shown. I likened it to an A-7 with an afterburner, without the projected map display, but much sexier. I was a one-man office until I hired Dick Jordan to be my NCO. We had worked together at Eglin. My boss, Lt Col Jerry Singleton, a test pilot, arrived a year later from Edwards AFB, California. According to Chief Master Sergeant Rufus Davis who worked in the Air Force Plant Representative Office (AFRRO) at General Dynamics, Dick Jordan called me Notes, because I took notes all the time. Rufus calls me "notes" to this day. I still make notes, except today I do it on my iPhone in the app they appropriately named after me — Notes. Rufus and I also share the same birthday, just not the same year — he's a real trooper at 87, and we never forget out birthdays.

I made a film for AFCMD (Air Force Contract Management Division) of the ATP process from takeoff to landing. Each flight had a T-38 chase plane to make sure everything was working ok from the outside view which the F-16 pilot could not see (gear up and locked, etc.) Jerry was the front Man, and Captain Harry Strittmatter was the main character.

I made one significant contribution to the safety of the airplane. To check the brake anti-skid system, we would stomp on the brakes as soon as we landed, about 120 knots. The system was designed to cycle to keep the brakes from locking while applying maximum braking. If the system failed it would chatter (I believe) for about one and a half seconds before locking the brakes. Well, to yours truly, that time frame seemed like milliseconds. One flight I did my normal procedure and the next thing I knew the right tire blew and the airplane turned 45 degrees to the right. I'm going down the runway facing the hangar buildings thinking "what the hell is wrong with this picture." My heart was in my throat, but I did what I was trained to do — undo what you just did. I got off the brakes, the nose swung around to face down the runway (much better picture), I engaged the nose wheel steering and flopped to a stop. I never will understand why the gear didn't collapse with the airplane going sideways down the runway. I was protected from above again. They redesigned the anti-skid system.

I had several unique opportunities in the F-16 program. The first was the chance to fly production models off the assembly line at SABCA, Gosselies, Belgium and Schiphol, Amsterdam, The Netherlands. I would go over for two weeks and either live in Brussels, Belgium, or Amsterdam. On one trip I made a side trip to Paris. I bought a few art pieces at Montmartre and visited Notre Dame and the Louvre among other things. What impressed me the most was the actual size of the Mona Lisa. The picture of it in my art book in grade school was bigger than the actual work.

Another adventure was flying an F-16 from Mildenhall, England to Langley AFB, Virginia in September 1980. The airplane was featured in the Farnborough air show. Jerry had flown the airplane over, and I met him in London after flying over from Fort Worth. He met me at my hotel, and we left to see the white cliffs of Dover. The first place we stopped enroute was at McDonalds in London to eat. Go figure. The flight home was 8.5 hours with just the tanker and me. I refueled multiple times enroute, the timing calculated so that I could make it to a divert base from my present location over the Atlantic. When I shut down the airplane at Langley, fuel started pouring out of the bottom of the airplane. Saved again.

The third special event was delivering an F-16 to Israel. We took four airplanes. While we were there, we received a three-day tour of the country. It was surreal to be in the place that I had been reading about in the Bible my entire life. To stand on the Mount of Olives, walk through the Garden of Gethsemane, stand at the Wailing Wall, eat fish at the Sea of Capernaum, and visit Bethlehem to name a few was mind blowing. It is perhaps the greatest trip I have ever taken.

Jerry and I had access to a great fishing hole by the plant on Lake Worth. One day I caught a five-pound catfish. I knew how to hold them to keep the daggers they had on each side of their head from stabbing you while you took the hook out. Not so fast — didn't matter. Quicker than the blink of an eye, the catfish impaled me in my hand between my thumb and forefinger. Good thing Jerry was there. He had to cut the pectoral fin off the catfish to release the two of us from each other, and then pull the fin out of my hand. He wanted to drive me to the Carswell base hospital to have the hand cleaned up. I said not necessary and went home to do it myself. I require a lot of maintenance.

A General Dynamics flight ops employee drove us to and from the airplanes every day. The F-16s were about a quarter mile from the ops buildings and it was about 110 degrees on this particular day. We had a short maintenance delay, so we waited in his air-conditioned car. Chuck was a short man, spoke with a stutter, and his parents had come to the US from Romania. Since we had no cell phones, I asked him what he did before he joined General Dynamics. He said he was in the Air Force and retired as a Chief Master Sergeant. Well, I knew they didn't give those away, being the top one percent of the enlisted force, so I asked him how he got in the Air Force. He said he joined in 1941 and was sent to the Philippines. Say what?

He then told his story of how he survived the Bataan death march, 36 days on a Japanese hell ship, and three and a half years in the Mukden POW camp. I was shocked again and turned to him and said, "I should be driving you." I have a frigging Bataan death march survivor driving me to my airplane. From that moment, Chuck Dragich was my hero and friend. I don't think anyone in the plant knew this story.

Since both my kids lived in the Dallas — Fort Worth area, after I retired, I would always visit Chuck and Ann Dragich when I went to see them. Over the next 20 years, I heard more gruesome details of his WWII incarceration experience. I was able to kid him that all that Bataan death march and POW stuff was just good training for him since he raised seven daughters. Eight women in the house and Chuck. I wasn't sure which was tougher.

Another adventure in Fort Worth was starting a company to publish a Researched Bible Guide (RBG). I had just completed a master's degree in business administration from the University of West Florida while at Eglin. Linda came up with the idea for the RBG (she taught English for a year after college before we got married) and she was the researcher. I got to put my newfound skills to use by incorporating the business, setting up the accounting books, the bulk rate postal mailing, typing, and proofing. As the Executive (Administrative) Officer at Homestead and Myrtle Beach I was blessed with the ability to proof-read, a skill which I despised but was good at.

When my assignment came to Headquarters (HQ) PACAF (Pacific Air Forces) at Hickam AFB, Hawaii, we had already moved the business out of the house into an office in Fort Worth. A church member became the manager for us. Our circulation was all over the US and several other countries in Europe, Asia, and Australia. Not a big enterprise, but one of the most rewarding and exciting things I had done aside from flying. I now had a retirement job in sight.

My four years in Fort Worth were amazing — a great job, with great people to work with, a lifetime of memories. I got promoted to

Major the second time around thanks to the support of all my bosses and the OER indorsement of General Baker. We were there from 1977 to 1981.

Chapter 9
Honolulu, Hawaii
(1982-1986)

I was assigned as the only F-16 Flight Safety Officer after completing the Accident Investigation Course at University of Southern California (USC). I have diplomas from everywhere. The HQ building is in one of the converted barracks from WW II. Its nickname was the Hickam Hotel, housing 3200 men in 14 wings. It was filled to capacity when it took 27 direct hits on December 7th, 1941. It still has the pock marks from the attack. It is part of the Hickam Field National Historic Landmark listed on the National Register in 1985.

My introduction to General O'Malley, CINC (Commander-in-Chief) PACAF was an awkward one. I was on the phone with the AF Safety Center in California hearing about an F-16 that had just crashed. The general walked into the safety office, and everyone came to attention, me with the phone in my ear. I didn't want to be rude to anyone, so while the general stood there waiting to greet me, I explained that I had to go because I had a four-star standing in front of me. I hung up, apologized to the general, shook hands, and was the first one to tell him the bad news. General Jeromy F. O'Malley was the one who endorsed my OER and got me promoted to Lt Col the second time around.

From the normal, everyday staff summary sheets and coordination, one in particular stands out. My claim to fame at HQ PACAF was a goal I set for the entire command. You might know that the safety office is not the prime destination at HQ PACAF — operations is.

As I settled into my job, I became aware that HQ PACAF had not won the annual Flight Safety award (for a small command) in 17 years. My brain was firing on all cylinders. I dug out my staff summary sheet and wrote a proposal to set a goal to win the award that year. I coordinated it through all the 14 wings of the building up to CINC PACAF, who I believe at the time was General Braswell. It was accepted and transmitted to all PACAF units. Damn if we didn't win the thing. I guess goal setting does have its moments and rewards. Who knew.

Once a month on Friday afternoon, the safety office would take off to play golf at a local par 3 course. I was not a golfer. The first Friday afternoon I found myself manning the office alone. The next Friday the same thing. My mama didn't raise no dummies. I'm a golfer! But not a conventional golfer. The class clown golfer.

On my first trip to the par 3 course, I was armed with a tennis racquet. I do play tennis. At Eglin AFB I won the AFSC (Air Force Systems Command) senior division twice in a row and was invited to try out for the Air Force team twice. They only took two seniors to the interservice tournament. I was always number three.

You can hit a golf ball far with a tennis racquet and pretty straight, too. It makes a funny sound. Putting is problematic. But I finished the course with a decent score.

The next month I applied my vast fishing skills. I drilled a hole in a golf ball, put a small eye screw in it, and attached it to my fishing line like you would a lure. Four-pound test works best. The golf ball is heavier than most lures and you can really cast that sucker a long way. Close to the green putting is a cinch. You just walk to the opposite side of the flag and reel that puppy into the hole. Voila! I think I birdied every hole. The troops were not amused,

The third Friday I was out of options and Col Phil Bowen, the Director of Safety, was out of patience. I used actual golf clubs, and my score suffered greatly. Oh well, such is life. You only live once.

I had my hair cut in the barber shop in the HQ building. Fred Shimabaku did a great job, but as the conversation changed to fishing, he became a mentor and leader in another great adventure. Schofield Barracks near Miliani Town in the middle of Oahu is home to the 25th Infantry Division. The army rangers train right there on a trail that is rated dangerous to treacherous. For real. Fred took me down this trail into a large stream at the bottom. It is an hour and a half trek down with a trail a foot and a half wide with shear drop offs of over 300 feet. You'd better watch your step and stay on the trail.

We took our fishing gear with us. The scene down there is spectacular, and I may be one of the few haoles (non-native Hawaiians) who has ever been there. It reminded me of the Philippine jungle. Fred showed me who to contact to get permission to use the trail. I took friends and family. They were impressed.

My stepson, Cord was certainly impressed. I took him on one trip and briefed him that it was a dangerous trail and to just throttle back the energy and not skip or jump along the trail. He was 15 or 16 so that advice went in one ear and out the other. As we descended on the trail, Cord was happily skipping and jumping around. Next thing he knew he was off the trail to the left. The trail is deceptive because the vegetation grows horizontally out from the trail about three feet with some small saplings among the brush. The trail looks like it might be four feet wide. Cord fell into the brush. I went to give him a hand to get back up on the trail, but he declined. He went to stand up and his

My first operational assignment at Ubon 1969-1970 – F-4D's

Bob Gomez (right) and me sitting on MK-82 500 popund bombs with fuse extenders loaded on an F-4D at Ubon, Thailand 1969-70

Night Owl F-4 refueliong from a KC-135 tanker over Laos

497th TFS Nite Owls, Ubon, Thailand 1970 – sitting on the wing,
left to right: Me, Warren Stewart, Fred Bieber, Bob Gomez

The Dog's Head

Top row: Dedad and my dad. Middle row: Nanny and my mom.
Front row: me and my brother Ken on mom's lap

USAFA doolie year 1963

Cadet parade uniform – USAFA 1963

A-7D's at Korat, Thailand

The five generation picture – Bob, Me and Dad in the back.
Nanny and Vincent in the middle

Ubon Thailand Wold Facs – bottom row third from the right

Enjoying a quite moment at the farm

Flight Foundation Cessna-152

Family members at the HOF (left to right) grandson Vincent, son Bill, Christine Wang friend of Jonathan, me, sister-in-law Penny, son Bob (Vincent's dad), brother Ken, nephew Jonathan

Veterans day program left to right: me, Richard Gomez, Austin Moody, Suzanne Gomey, Ethan Gomez wearing Bob's shirt, and Holly Gomez

The 'boys' ready to leave the cabin at Kishkutena

A typical photo of a school group at the airport for Orientation Flights

A classroom unlike any other in the school

Arlington National Cemetery

Our cadets laying the wreath at the Tomb of the Unknown Soldier

Field trip to Washington DC

Inside the Air Force Museum

Our solo cadets get to wear flight suits instead of BDUs

Couples left to right: My dad and mon (Bob & Carlyn)
Dedad and Nanny, Uncle Herb and Glenna

legs went straight down through the brush, being held up only by his arms from the shoulders to the elbows. I asked again if I could help him. He accepted. I pulled him up on the trail. Funny how there was no more jumping or skipping the rest of the day. Another great teaching moment. I don't think we told Phillis about that incident, in case Cord wanted to get permission to go on the trail again. She's probably old enough now to handle it. I hope I am.

On one trip with Fred, he injured his leg while we were fishing, and it was getting late in the evening. He could not hike back up the trail. What to do. Two options. One, spend the night and have the families worried and contact the President of the United States to get help, or two, carry Fred out of there. We decided to try and make it out. I was the engine and Fred was the caboose. He held on to my belt and I hiked up the trail pulling Fred along. All he had to do was keep taking steps.

As it got dark, the trail was a darker shade of grey/black than the weeds. I poked my fishing pole ahead of me on the trail just to make sure it was solid ground. I knew there was a four-foot deep and one-foot-wide ditch across the trail about two thirds of the way up. By the time we got there I could see where the ditch was and when I poked, there was nothing there. We took one break for about 2 minutes on the way up. Typically, just walking out alone, we would take several longer breaks. We got to the top of the trail just as it turned pitch black. We had made it. Fred and I hugged each other knowing we had cut it to the second. He grabbed my legs and said: "you have very strong legs". In that instant I did, but it just shows what adrenaline, heart, and mind can do when required. And, how great it is to stay in shape every day. Another non-bucket list adventure checked off.

Another stab through the heart occurred during this tour. I was TDY (on a business trip) to the mainland and took the opportunity to visit my folks in Woodbridge. VA. Mom handed me a letter from Linda addressed to me, but mailed to their house. That was strange. Everybody reading this book gets it, but I didn't. Even worse, it was devastating. She told me she was moving back to Fort Worth and taking the kids. WTFO? Long story short, when I returned to Hawaii, I had to get a ride home from my boss, Lt Col Bob Hadley, to a house with no kids and half the furniture. WTFO? This was Pearl Harbor (which was only a few miles away from Mililani Town) all over again. The word divorce had never been spoken by either one of us our entire lives. So much for my astute military prowess. Life is certainly unpredictable.

Chapter 10
My Savior Cometh
(1984-1986)

The next six months were spent with lawyers, court hearings in Texas, negotiations, etc. I finally had to give Linda the business and the house to keep my retirement. And I was still four years from retirement. Anyway, I lost my wife, kids, business and house in the blink of an eye.

I mentioned I played tennis. One of my tennis "buddies" was Linda, the wife of a Navy Commander. She knew a "gal" who was single. When Dave, her husband, made Captain, she had a party at their house and invited both of us.

Phillis didn't know it was a set up. She walked in and there was a hush among the crowd. Someone said, "There she is, whataya think". We hung out at the party and then went to her house to hang out some more. She was really pretty, had a son Cord, and we set up another date at a restaurant on the north shore. We came back from dinner to my place and turned on the TV. She gave me three choices — Nachos, TV, or me. I guess I made the right choice.

Phillis Fox took Cord on a two-week trip to Europe (instead of paying her income tax — another story) and asked me to house sit their African Gray parrot. I did and never left. The townhouse was very painful with all the memories and reminders of my past 16 years. I rented it and eventually sold it.

Living in Kailua and travelling across the Pali every day to and from work was idyllic. After a year or two it became "normal" and I had to remind myself how special this was. I bought a wind surfer, and Cord and I took lessons. After work several times a week we would load the wind surfer on top the car and drive a few minutes to Kailua beach and wind surf for a few hours. Throw in a few deep-sea fishing trips and life was good.

We were married in the base chapel with just a best man, Phil Bowen, and bridesmaid, Carkey Ainley, on 17 January 1986. It pleases me to no end that she has to ask me what date we got married. And I remember. Too bad she doesn't forget everything I've done wrong over the past 37 years.

She literally saved my life. Ever since hitting that tree, flying and working had been a challenge mentally and physically due to my apparent inability to handle the regret and stress of that moment. She would just say "don't worry about it." Fortunately, I listened. I went to a psychologist, left the church where I had been Chairman of the Board — briefly — and tried to just become a regular joe bag of donuts.

I have to thank my church family again for getting me through this ordeal. From the time Linda left, the Wenkes and Higgins were special. The Higgins invited me to join the Honolulu Barbershop Chorus. That was another new, non-bucket list adventure that I checked off. It was very therapeutic. It lasted about a year until my adventure with Phillis trumped my singing career.

Phillis was just what the doctor ordered. She was carefree and vivacious — everything I wasn't. We complimented each other.

Nothing in common. Perfect, it worked. The way she tells it, I said "marry me, marry me, and we'll never leave Hawaii". That's her fairytale.

She knew nothing about the military. At my Lt Col promotion party at the O'Club at Hickam, she went up to a two-star general and asked him if that meant "twice a colonel". And they still kept me on the list.

On our second date to the Punahou carnival in downtown Honolulu, we got stuck in traffic with two kids in the back (Cord and his best friend Billy) and she got sick and there was no place to go. She grabbed my jacket, put it under her butt and had an episode to write a book about. She did not want to get her new car seat messy. The two boys in the back stood up and stuck their heads out of the open sunroof and yelled "my mom just took a dump in the car." Fun stuff. I married her anyway.

During my tour at Headquarters Pacific Air Forces (PACAF) I did a fair amount of travelling from Hawaii to Korea, Japan, and one trip to Pakistan. General Brad Hosmer took a group of officers to brief at the Pakistan Air War College in Karachi. My role was to brief A-10 capabilities. We arrived in Karachi after spending a night in Bangkok, Thailand. The uniform for the briefing was dress blues. I went to find my uniform in my hangup bag, and it was inconceivably not there. I looked everywhere — even in my dop kit but it would not appear. Embarrassing moment number 267. I did the briefing in my coat and tie. We were introduced to a prominent store owner of Persian rugs. I purchased two rugs and still own one.

On one of my TDYs to Seoul, Korea, Phillis joined me for a Christmas shopping spree. We made a group trip to Panmunjom at the Demilitarized Zone (DMZ) between North and South Korea. We had to sign a form acknowledging that this was a dangerous place and there had been over 450 border incidents since the treaty was signed. I was in my uniform and had many pictures taken of me by the North Koreans. We got to walk into the room where the 1953 Korean Armistice Agreement that ended the Korean War was signed. We walked around the table which put us into North Korea. Two weeks after we were there, another border incident occurred where the instigator was killed.

We spent several amazing days in Seoul. The South Koreans really love Americans. It was very comforting and gratifying. One of their traditions is that, if a shop keeper makes a sale to the first customer of the day, they will have a good sales day. We found that out when we happened to be the first customer in a jewelry store. They would not let us leave until we purchased something for dirt cheap. Next day we set our alarms for 0400. We would have made out like a bandit had we only bought for ourselves. The prices were so cheap that we bought members only leather jackets (remember those) for the entire family — like six of them. Same for shoes, duffle style bags, luggage of all types, jewelry, and ski outfits. We even had several pieces of antique furniture shipped home. We paid $5,000 for $300 worth of items that we needed. But everyone had a very merry Christmas.

On another TDY to Seoul in December of 1983, I was really into the Christmas spirit and was led one evening to write the following poem. Like this book, it just came to me exactly as I wrote it from start to finish. Here it is.

What's In a Gift?

Gifts come in all sizes,
Are bought by the hordes,

Packaged in great splendor,
They are fit for Lords.

Sent to common folk,
Middle class, and kings,
They books 'n banjos,
And records and rings.

Opened by infants,
Teenagers and adults,
All the eyes sparkle
When they see the results.

Unwrap all your gifts,
And you'll surely find,
Behind it a story
Of a special kind.

First thing to undo
Is that plastic band,
Telling us it came
From a faraway land.

The brown paper is easy
To tear off in a jif,
It's obvious from the size
It's not a car or a skiff.

The cardboard box is aged,
Like a vintage wine.
It reveals its contents
In a very short time.

Ah, many packages,
All wrapped in bright paper.
We can now tear into them,
Like a detective on a caper.

A pretty bow, scotch
Tape and some ribbon,
All is removed,
But something is hidden.

The gift is in sight,
But what does it say,
About the events
That led to this day.

When the giver was
Walking to and fro,
And looking in stores
Numb from head to toe.

It speaks of a character.
Akin to the Christ.
It says of this person,
They're kind of nice.

The Bible will tell us
If we look into James,
The truth about gifts,
On a much higher plain.

Every perfect gift
Comes from above.

It whispers, "My child,
You have all my love."

And the love that's expressed,
In the gifts that you see,
Is the pure love of God
Shining through you and me.

So open your gifts
And let your thoughts climb.
Be aware in your hearts,
That it's Christmas time.

When Phillis found out we were to be transferred to the mainland, she called someone (thank heavens I don't know who) and said she wanted me assigned to the Space Program in Colorado Springs. The person on the other end of the line politely said, "Ma'am, that's not how this works."

I was assigned to Eglin AFB again, this time to the Tactical Air Warfare Center (TAWC) as the TAC liaison to the Systems Command AMRAAM (Advanced Medium Range Air-to-Air Missile) SPO (System Program Office). Now you know why we use tons of acronyms.

Chapter 11
Eglin AFB Again
(1986-1990)

This would be my last assignment. We bought a new house in Niceville, formerly called Boggy Bayou. I made a name for myself here also. As a desk jockey, I was the only TAC member assigned to the SPO, commanded by a one-star. They had a staff meeting every morning at 0730 with about 15 Colonels and Lieutenant Colonels around the large conference table. I sat in the middle of the table right inside the door to the room from the hall. After a year or so, I was informed that the staff meeting was changed to 0600. Are you kidding me? I had a brilliant plan. The next morning, after waking up at oh-dark-thirty, I stood outside the door waiting for the general and his staff to be seated. I had on my pajama top over my uniform, I mussed up my hair (which I still had then), staggered into the room and slumped into my chair. There was dead silence. Then the place erupted into applause. That was the first and last 0600 staff meeting. Didn't have to say a word.

General Jaquish was the TAWC Commander, a three-star. My golf game hadn't improved much, and Phillis didn't have one, but we played every time there was a TAWC golf event. General Jaquish always had Phillis in his foursome. Certainly not because she was a good or even poor golfer. Probably because she was the life of the party and he enjoyed her colorful commentary on what a stupid game golf was and wanted to keep an eye on the renegade wife. She had a great time — mostly for the stories she could tell years later of her adventures on the golf course. If she ever writes a book, I'm in trouble.

Eventually I became Chief of the Air-to-Air Weapons Division. I had a great boss and friend in Col Bob Byran or bullet as he was known. Cord went to Florida State where he crammed four years of education into five and would have taken longer had we not pulled the plug on his funding. We did manage to take in a football game, see Deion Sanders play, and get beer spilled down our backs in the student section.

I also had great people working for me. There were two analysts who had to go to the White Sands Missile Range (WSMR) in New Mexico to analyze the missile data. They had complained for years that it would be so much better to do the analysis at Eglin. Through a friend from my earlier tour at Eglin, I was able to procure money to buy the test equipment so they could do the analysis right there at Eglin. They were ecstatic and like kids in a candy store. One of my goals during each assignment was to leave the unit in better shape than when I got there. I hope that was the case.

One test mission took us to California for about two weeks. All I remember is that I had to do laundry, and the laundromat was in a seedy part of town. I went to the very back to do the laundry. Everyone else in there was Hispanic. I heard someone come in the door and start telling people he had just gotten off a boat from Venezuela. He was asking for money. I did not want to have to deal with this. By the time he got to me in the back, I had a plan. He told me the same story and I said "Ich kann sie nicht verstehen" (I don't understand you — in German). My Academy classes paying off again. He asked again and I gave the same answer. He had this incredulous look on his face — I'm the only Caucasian in the laundromat and I don't speak English. He then said, "You don't understand me, do you." I had to choke back my response which was to say "no." I just stood there and looked at him, and he walked away. If I had said no, I may have been knifed.

I retired on 1 January 1991. The ceremony in December was presided over by Col Harry Johnson. Harry, Mike Lang, and I had been roommates at Korat in the A-7. Too many stories to tell here. But what a pleasure and honor for me to have my warrior friend by my side when I retired. The three of us have kept in touch ever since.

I don't remember much of what I said at the end of the ceremony. What I do remember is reaching back up under the inside back of my Class A Jacket and pulling an 8x10 color photo from a safety pin, and proudly displaying the picture of my first grandson to the crowd. Vincent Carl Powley was born in August of 1990, just 5 months before my retirement. I was a proud grandpa for the first time, and another sucker was born into the fishing legacy.

Since this was Christmas, the family had come to Fort Walton Beach to see me retire. We took advantage of that to take a five-generation picture — my grandmother, my dad, me, my son, and my new grandson. It was the only time we were all together.

Chapter 12
Six Months Foot Loose and Fancy Free
(January-July 1991)

What to do now. The first thing was to test my tennis skills in the USTA (United States Tennis Association) over 45 in Florida. My intermittent tennis coach, Raudel Barba, thought I should make it in the top 20. I played several tournaments around the state. Most notable was in Jacksonville where there was a drive-by shooting just a block from the tennis courts. WTFO. It was a fun time. My best win was against the number 6 player in the state (I was unranked), I ended up ranked number 17. Raudel was spot on. Lots of good tennis players in Florida.

Phillis got me into stained glass in Hawaii. We got halfway decent at it, and I presented a stained glass HQ PACAF patch to the safety office when I left. Now we were into pottery. I envy the jewelers. They show up at a craft fair with a briefcase with $20,000 worth of merchandise. Potters, on the other hand, must pack as if they were on a PCS (Permanent Change of Station) move every time they go to and come back from a craft fair. Just like golf, after a few craft fairs of packing, setting up, packing, doing most of the grunt work, I became a potter. Phillis was the real deal, throwing on the wheel. I did slab and extrusions which was simpler but still allowed you to express your artistic talent, which I had in un-abundance. The key is the glaze and the firing. It's like Christmas every time you open the kiln. Some are magnificent, some you have to throw away and try again. We both ended up having our pottery sold in shops from Berea, Kentucky to Buford, South Carolina, as well as locally.

One thing that I did which didn't earn me many brownie points, was to take my new-found extra time to organize all the chemicals used in the glazing of the pottery. Phillis would keep them around the wheel and knew exactly where they were. I, on the other hand, had to search continuously to find them. That would not do. So, I organized all the chemicals alphabetically and put them on shelves in the garage where we worked.

Well, I wish you could have heard the words of praise (not) from Phillis. She will tell you the story today, decades later, of how her idiot husband organized the chemicals and she had to undo it, so she knew where they were. Oh well, best laid plans…

I was not getting much traction from my airline applications. The combination of the hiring demographics, fighter time only, and lack of recent currency put me out of the window. At one of the craft fairs, I met a fellow retiree at a booth who expounded on the joys of being an Air Force Junior Reserve Officer Training Corps (AFJROTC) instructor. There's those wonderful, short, acronyms again. I threw my hat in the ring and made my application.

My first interview was in Erwin, Tennessee for Unicoi County High School. Ellis Murphy, the Principal, interviewed me. I was the seventh potential candidate he had interviewed. The JROTC unit was on probation, and I suggested "let's take 'em flyin" to get them excited about something and recruit more students. They hired me.

Chapter 13
Unicoi County High School
Erwin, Tennessee (1991-2001)

We rented our house in Niceville and came to Unicoi County in August 1991. We were fortunate to find a rental house thanks to Dave Byrd. My first meeting with the Superintendent of Schools, Dr. Ronnie Wilcox, was a few days later. During the meeting he told me he was thinking of cancelling the JROTC program. Say what? Nice time to tell me. Now I know what it feels like to have the rug pulled out from under you. Fortunately, I had read the contract between HQ AFJROTC at Maxwell AFB, Alabama, and the school system. It required a year's advance notice. I had bought myself at least a one-year job. The unit is still there today.

One of the first afternoons we were there, Ellis invited us over to his house for a barbeque. He was hosting a high school team for a job well done and we met his wife Doris, an art teacher at the high school. Phillis, a real estate agent on Oahu, is now in the mountains of upper east Tennessee, having been rescued from paradise by me. One of her first conversations with Ellis involved asking him what they did around here for entertainment. Ellis responded, "That's kind of a personal question, isn't it?" They were fast friends from then on.

While moving into the rental house, I had a surreal moment. The only item that I had from the cottage at Laurel Lake was an old, probably Sears and Roebuck, wind-up mantel clock that had been on the mantel above the fireplace. I had shipped it with us on every move from 1967 to now. I would put the clock on a shelf or a mantel, if we had one, and wind it up. It would not run. I took it several times over the two decades to get it "fixed." It never ran. I unpacked it and put it on a shelf in one of the rooms. I turned and walked away without doing anything to it, and several seconds later I heard it chime. It has worked ever since. I guess it was happy to come home to the mountains. I can't explain it.

My proposal to have a flying program was presented by Ronnie to the school board. He must have worked some magic behind the scenes because the school board voted 4-3 to accept the proposal. One vote does make a difference. It led to our recognition as the top aerospace science program in the nation twice and my motivation to write this book. Awesome!

Ronnie introduced me to the Erwin Kiwanis club and invited me to join. Best thing I could have done as a newbie in Erwin. The first meeting I attended on a Tuesday at noon was in the basement of the Elms restaurant. I was wearing my flight suit. I sat down and Fain Bennett came over to see who this military guy was. His wife Linda had been an Army nurse, and he was familiar with military life. He introduced himself and we have been best friends and partners in the flight program ever since. He guided me through the translation from military jargon to education speak. He's a people person and has helped me read people and situations and understand "what the captain means."

Funny — or not so funny story. Ronnie took me fishing one afternoon on the Nolichucky River. We parked my truck, walked to the river and waded out. We fished as we worked our way downstream. When we quit a few hours later, we decided to get out of the river and cut through the woods to get to the truck. About 30 yards into our trek, we walked through a yellow-jackets nest. We both yelled and lit out of there. About 50 yards further we walked through another nest. Holly crap. By the time we got to the truck we both had about seven stings. As I drove back home, he gave me some chewing tobacco to put in my gums to moisten, and then put on the sting. It worked. Learn something new every day — a lesson I hope not to repeat. Fun times!

On one of our trips back to Florida to check on the rental house, we brought some items back to Tennessee. There were some shelving units for our pottery displays at the craft fairs that we had to strap to the roof of our new, red Jeep Cherokee four-wheel drive that we desperately needed in east Tennessee. We stopped for gas on the way home and with the fill-up came a free car wash. You got it. Phillis and I decided to take advantage of this generous offer. It was an automatic-type car wash. We drove in to the appropriate place, and let the brushes and sprayers do their thing. What the hell was all that racquet. We looked at each other in horror as we realized our mistake. Nothing to do about it now. We pulled out with the cleanest shelving in the history of the world. I inspected the roof and its contents. Everything seemed to be normal with no apparent damage to the Jeep. Guess I tied them on pretty good.

My first field trip with the students was an eye opener. We went to a Braves baseball game in Atlanta. A friend of mine went along as a chaperone. We watched the game and then went to a motel. The worst night of my life. The kids had been drinking and were crawling on top of the bus and running around the pool after curfew. I had to sit outside on the lounge chairs by the pool to keep them inside. I fell asleep. Don't know what they did, but when we got back to school the principal called me in because the kids accused me of being drunk. I told him I didn't drink. I have a history of not drinking and called

Harry Johnson to have him tell Ellis I don't drink. Welcome to teaching. It's a small town. I'm sure some still think I was drunk. Les said he would never go on another trip again. Don't blame him!

I learned a lot about field trips from that experience and ever since then, after call-to-quarters, the doors were taped, and they were not to come out of their rooms until the tape was removed at a specified time in the morning. Worked great for 22 years except for a trip to Charleston which I can't comment on. FBI, CIA and all that stuff. Nothing is foolproof with teenagers.

We had a special rule that the only time you could use the elevators in the motel was checking in or out with luggage. Otherwise use the stairs, including instructors. I do the same thing when I travel alone — not with Phillis. Worked great every time. The only challenge was on one trip when they put us on the seventh floor. That was tough, but rules are rules. The kids hated it, but it was great exercise. Really made you take inventory before you left the room. Going back was rarely an option.

Rescuing Phillis from Hawaii put me on her permanent shit-list, where I remain today. Not possible to redeem yourself when you take someone from paradise where they lived for 18 years — even if they do love you. Great news for me — Phillis loves the mountains. As an artist, she appreciates the constant beauty and scenery and wildlife the area presents every day.

The indigenous people are a little different. The first thing Ellis did to welcome me to UCHS was give me a jar of moonshine. Cool. Too bad I don't drink but I did have a sip just to be polite. The first Apple Festival, a tradition held the first weekend in October, Phillis and I went to check it out. One of my students was coming toward us wearing a trench coat. He wanted to show me something. He opened his coat and there were cherry bombs, knives, guns, you name it, on each side of the coat. Phillis commented "what the hell have we gotten ourselves into." It's been a dream come true.

I had three rules that I displayed prominently in front of the classroom every day since I started teaching. Rule #1 — Respect. Rule #2 — Deeds Not Words. Rule #3 — No Excuses. Six words. Kids can quote them decades after graduation. My take on it to them was, follow all these rules and I can almost guarantee you will be successful in life. Violate any one of them and I can almost guarantee you won't. Has worked for me.

One such example is Austin Moody, a four-year AFJROTC cadet and private pilot. The confidence he gained from his flying experience gave him the courage to go to Nashville after high school and pursue his dream of becoming a country singer. I was blown away when, at the age of 25, he volunteered to do benefit concerts in his hometown of Kingsport for FLIGHT Foundation. Most people don't think of that until they are in their seventies, if ever. I was also impressed when I saw his name tag on his flight suit. Under his name it said, "No Excuses." He is living proof of the rules.

His first concert was at the Johnson City Country Club, where we held a Christmas dinner to celebrate our success over the past year. Attendees were mainly JROTC instructors from the schools who participated in the Flight Orientation Program (FOP) program, mentors of the program, parents and their solo students. One year we had Lt Col Chuck O'Donnell, an AFJROTC and flight instructor from Knoxville attend as the entertainment. He was the lead singer in a barbershop quartet. He let me update my barbershop singing by joining them as lead in 'My Wild Irish Rose."

Phillis and I continued our pottery when we purchased 10 acres of land in Unicoi County which is now the town of Unicoi. It had an old house that was pretty much in ruin, so we did our pottery in the house. Some mornings you would walk in and see rat tracks in the clay that was still damp, waiting to dry. Phillis had one order for 100 mugs and 25 casserole dishes for an ETSU nursing school function. She completed the order, suffered some carpal tunnel symptoms and decided, as an artist, she liked doing creative things better than mass production. Several years later I spent three years tearing down the old house so we could build a rental house there. I thought I might find something valuable in the walls of the old house, but the only thing of interest was a block of scrap wood in the walls that I was going to throw out until I turned it over and found writing saying: "this house was buylt (his spelling) by H P Phillips January 8, 1884." At least I knew how old it was. We had saved the hand-hewn barn, which was probably built in the early 1800s, but the house was too far gone. All the pottery equipment was stored in the barn.

Not to worry, Phillis had new plans. We, as in she and then me, took up bee keeping. We had several hives, had the outfits, and went to beekeeper's meetings. The bees are actually pretty fascinating. To smoke the hive and be able to open it and sweep bees off the combs and have them not care a lick is something else. Phillis won a blue ribbon at the Appalachian Fair Grounds for one of her honey-filled combs.

It became very difficult to keep the hives alive in the winter and after having to re-queen the hives we went down to one hive and then none. The other factor is that Phillis is deathly allergic to bee stings. She had to call 911 and go to the hospital because of a wasp sting. Scary stuff. She always carries an EpiPen.

Chapter 14
The Flight Program
(1991-present)

After the school board approved our flying program with a 4-3 vote, I took the first cadet up, Aaron Byrd, plus Charlie Edwards from The Erwin Record, a local newspaper, on 15 May 1992. Dot Evans owned the flight school at TRI-cities airport in Blountville, TN, Aero Flight, and sponsored our first flight for $100. We flew in a Cessna 172 and the event was covered by WJHL channel 11 TV (CBS).

Airplanes don't fly due to lift; they fly due to money. To fund the program, we started taking three students on one-hour flights over houses and businesses in Unicoi County. I would circle the property and take pictures with a view and then close-up. Once the film was developed, I would pick the best wide-angle view and close-up and have them enlarged to 5x7. I made a folder with 16 pictures in plastic covers, with a cover sheet that said Compliments of Unicoi County High School AFJROTC. I would then visit the prospective sponsor and ask if they would donate $100 to the cadet flight program. I would spend at least an hour talking about the program. It took a lot of time. But we raised $8,000 (80 sponsors) which kept us in the air.

I became aware of a group in California at the Aims Research Center that would help fund aviation related programs for kids. I found a number and Mark Leon answered. I gave him my pitch and he said he didn't think he could help. Six months later I repeated the call with similar results. Six months later I did it again. Mark said, "You're not going to quit calling until I give you money. are you?" I said nope. He gave us $10,000 and that is what started us off on our path to stardom. Now we could fly15-20-minute flights instead of hour flights. Our productivity tripled.

Fain Bennett was so impressed with our program that he required his son Seth to take at least one semester of AFJROTC. Seth and his best friend Justin did so. Fain also sponsored both cadets for their solo. Seth was my first and Justin my second high school solo student. Seth stayed in JROTC, became my squadron commander his senior year, went to the Air Force Academy, and just made full Colonel (O-6).

This is the unique part of the program. A solo-only high school program. I can't think of too many better ways to instill confidence in a 16 or 17-year-old than flying an airplane by themselves. I have witnessed this now hundreds of times with parents, family members, teachers, and friends at the airport observing this adventure. It is a life-long memory — a real spike in their life.

Phillis has always said that the real impact of this program was that instead of coming to school with their heads down and thinking they may be trapped into the only way of life they knew, they now looked skyward to see so many possibilities, now which included flying.

In 1998 we formed a non-profit 501-C(3) corporation called Flight Lesson Instructional Grants Helping Teens (FLIGHT) Foundation. I spent two weeks trying to think of an appropriate, catchy name. Then I was in the bathroom relieving pressure on my brain and the words just flashed across my mind like a tickertape, No shit. True story.

Col Tom Reeves, a Vietnam helicopter pilot, and Distinguished Service Cross recipient (downgraded from the Medal of Honor), put me in touch with Retired Navy Captain Fred Vogt, Director of Aeronautics in the State Department of Transportation in Nashville. Fred and I met a few months later, and after discussing our mutual admiration for the F-4 Phantom II which we both had flown, we discussed the flight program. Obviously, Fred and I had an immediate connection as fighter pilots, and he liked the program enough to have us brief the Aeronautics Commissioners to get their approval for funding.

I had half a dozen solo students give the presentation — not me — and they were magnificent. Just blew them away. We had prepared and rehearsed at school. They sold the program because the program was about them. The board approved a $10,000 grant. The next year Brigadier General Bob Woods took over for Fred. We had a dozen wonderful years with Bob and his wife Wanda and my project manager Belinda Hampton. The grants increased over the years to a max of $88,000 at one point and for the 15 years they funded the program it was over $550,000. I'd say the cadets did a great job.

Fain and I always talked about the "magic bullet." The magic bullet was the fact that I was a teacher in the school system and not an "outsider." This gave me access to 26 high schools with JROTC programs — Army, Navy, Marines, and Air Force.

The instructors would bring a bus loaf of cadets to the airport to fly as a "field trip". We could get up to 30 students flown in under four hours. We now average over 600 students a year.

The solo program was very rigorous. I made up a solo packet consisting of a three-ring notebook, FAA's Airplane Flying Handbook, the Cessna-152 Pilot's Information Manual, and a logbook. I went through the FAA publication and made up a series of 450 sentences with missing words into six chapters, which comprised the ground school for the first six flight lessons. This took 24 hours of actual work time. I spread it out over a week.

The notebook contained this ground school material, completed by the students at home by filling in the missing words in each sentence. This way I knew they had read the material. It also contained the nine flight lessons, and everything else you needed to know to complete your solo, including flight physical information, memorization, traffic pattern diagram, pre-solo written tests, IACRA procedures for obtaining their student pilot's license, etc.

I would meet with the parents and student to go over the program to make sure we were all on the same page. In most cases, this was at a restaurant halfway between our homes. There were three contracts to sign and one had to be notarized. This outlined the scholarship requirements, student requirements to include keeping a journal of each flight, writing a thank you letter to the organization that provided their scholarship money, and reimbursement of scholarship money if things went awry. At the end of the solo, I would get the package back to refill it for the next student. They would keep their logbook, get a solo certificate, and a FLIGHT Foundation solo shirt that they were required to wear once a week to school. This was our advertisement for the program.

In the past 30 years there have been hundreds of sponsors/donors, but a few deserve special recognition. One of my first contacts at Greeneville Airport. where I do 95 percent of my flying, was Scott Niswonger. Scott is a businessman and philanthropist. He has been a mentor to me for decades, provided funds for extraordinary expenses not covered by grants, and for the purchase of a Cessna-152 for the Foundation. He is also an inductee into the Tennessee Aviation Hall of Fame. He has been flying since he was 16 years old — longer than I have but he is younger.

Those donations of $10,000 or more include NASA, Impact Plastics (Gerry O'Connor), and Paul & June Rossetti. Over $50,000 includes Scott Niswonger and a new State Partnership Grant. Donations/grants over $100,000 include the previous grants from the Tennessee Aeronautics Division, FedEx, and the Ray Foundation.

Chapter 15
Sullivan South High School
Kingsport, Tennessee (2001-2015)

In 2001, the Air Force opened a new JROTC unit in Sullivan County. Sullivan East and North both had Navy units. The principal at Sullivan South wanted me to bring my flight program to his school so he held out for an Air Force unit. I accepted and began another great adventure with my new ASI (Aerospace Science Instructor) Don Shawver who transferred from Virginia High. We both had experience.

We converted the electrical workshop into a great JROTC classroom. There was room for two large classrooms, two offices, and a supply/storage room. We had an outside door that led right to a drill area, and we didn't have to disturb any other classes. A perfect set-up,

We opened our doors in August 2001. We began recruiting the year before and flew some prospective cadets that summer. We took five rising seniors to a summer leadership school at McGhee-Tyson Air National Guard Base in Knoxville. They became our leadership cadre for the first year.

It took six years to bring the UCHS unit off probation to become a Distinguished Unit. We were a distinguished unit every year thereafter due to our flying program and the work of my ASI Mel Cooper. The first year at South we were a distinguished unit, one of only two in the country for first year programs. It helped to have experienced instructors (most new units start with new instructors) and the flight program. It also helped that Don Shawver, my fellow instructor, was so passionate about doing over 100 activities with the cadets every year including field trips, celebration picnics at the end of each year, random acts of kindness, orienteering, drill, color guard and physical fitness competitions, color guard and chorus at professional baseball and ice hockey games, Veteran's Day programs, military balls, award banquets, marching in parades for special events, taking the cadets to summer leadership schools for a week every summer, and manning the classroom while I was out flying.

Speaking of flying, the theme of the entire unit was flying. One of the homework assignments for the incoming freshmen was to make a model airplane that we could hang from the ceiling. When you walked into the classroom, you were awestruck by the décor of the entire room. It was home and a haven for many students. In the back classroom which we used as a multipurpose staff/work/storage room, we hung the shirts along the top of the wall just below the ceiling. We had over sixty shirts hanging along two walls of the room.

When a student was in solo training, they were issued a flight suit and could wear that one day a week instead of their BDUs, the military work uniform instead of the blue dress uniform. At one point we had seven cadets wearing their flight suits. When we were recognized as the best aerospace science program for high schools in the nation, we took the nomination package, a notebook, and presented it to the Director of Schools, Jubal Yennie, and the school board.

Another key to our success was that we had the best parent booster club in the world. Those guys were phenomenal. They would make all the arrangements for the military ball, decorate, provide food, and anything else that needed to be done. All I had to do was show up, and

I did that extremely well. They also shuttled cadets to the TRI-Cities airport in Blountville, not far from the school, so they could participate in the flight program during their AFJROTC class, a block of one hour and 45 minutes, and not miss any other classes. That allowed us to fly as much as we wanted and keep the other teachers happy.

I made it a practice to take the guidance counselors, Principal, other staff members, Director of Schools, and central office personnel flying. This would give them first-hand knowledge of what the program was about and, if enthusiastic, help direct students into the cadet program. Each flight would consist of letting the students experience zero g's, two g's, and a simulated dive bomb run. When I had the Director of Schools up, I held the two g turn until he agreed to a pay raise. Brent Palmer, the band director at Sullivan South, went up and became one of my few adult solo students and got his private pilot's license.

Somewhere in the second year, the school board received an anonymous letter asking about liability insurance — the ugly "L" word. We were shut down taking kids from class to the airport for the rest of the year until we found insurance to cover the gap between the $100,000 flight school insurance and the $250,000 per person insurance required by the school system. We had a guardian angel who wrote a stand-alone policy of $1,000,000 per event and $250,000 per person for the entire 11,000 student body for $1,200 a year. Fantastic. We were back in business.

The beginning of the recognition for how special this program was started in 2010, when I received the A. Scott Crossfield Award as the top high school aerospace science teacher in the nation. Seth Bennett, my first solo student, nominated me. I went to the ceremony at Wright-Patterson AFB in Dayton, Ohio. I met Sally Farley, Scott's daughter. Her son Justin and Walter Boyne presented the award. It was a special evening.

The ceremony was held in the Air Force Museum near the Vietnam aircraft exhibit. Looking at all the airplanes I had flown, I noticed the A-7 on display was a Myrtle Beach airplane and I wrote the tail number down. When I got home, I looked at my logbook and found out that I had flown that airplane. Guess I made at least one good landing. I have kept in contact with Sally ever since and continue to give her credit for all my subsequent awards. This was the catalyst for all the rest.

Let me illustrate. That same year, the Tennessee Aviation Hall of Fame (HOF) created a special award called the Tennessee Aviation Person of the Year award to recognize me for winning the Crossfield award. The next year, 2011, I received Tennessee's highest aviation recognition, the Career Contributions to Aviation Award, and in 2013 was inducted into the Tennessee Aviation HOF. See what I mean.

My workout buddy, James Smith, had a bucket list that included running Currahee, the three miles up, three miles down run made famous in the book and mini-series Band of Brothers. I said sure, that makes all this running have a purpose. I made it a JROTC event, and we took 5 cadets. After the run, we were taking pictures and this older gentleman drives up, gets out and asks what we were doing. I was 65 at the time and said we had just run Currahee. He said are you crazy — not the first time I've heard that — and I said why do you think that. Well, he knew what it was like to run Currahee at the age of 18, and it's tougher than the one in the movie. He then told us how he had joined a new form of warfare known as parachute infantry as a charter member of the 101st Airborne Division "Screaming Eagles" - trained at Toccoa, Georgia in the summer — had a free trip to England — jumped into Normandy on D-Day — got wounded —

jumped into Holland during Operation Market Garden — was at Bastogne for the hit drama series "Battle of the Bulge" - fought his way across Germany to capture the Eagles Nest at Berchtesgaden and end WW II in Europe — had an all-expenses paid trip back to America on the Queen Mary, and marched down Sachs Fifth Avenue in New York City to a ticker tape parade. I was speechless. Captain Richard Little had just made this event an absolutely epic adventure. He became a friend of mine and AFJROTC. He wrote me a letter in response to my request for some pictures and stated that this was the first time he had ever told that story in 65 years. I called to tell him about my good news regarding the FIHOF, and wish him a happy 98th birthday.

One day I was in Office Depot buying some supplies for the classroom when I found myself standing in line behind a gentleman having copies made. Being curious, I glanced over his shoulder and noticed that the copies were of certificates for medals — like The Distinguished Flying Cross. This intrigued me so I introduced myself and found out I was talking to Dempsey Morgan, a Tuskegee Airman.

We exchanged contact information. Dempsey and his wife Adrienne came to our classroom several times over the next few years to talk about his experiences. He also attended our award banquets to present the Tuskegee Award to a deserving cadet. That cadet will have a story to tell for the rest of their life.

When you see the iconic picture of the Tuskegee airmen kneeling in front of the wing looking forward and the pilot on the left looking to the right, that pilot is Dempsey Morgan. He spent the rest of his life in service to his faith and teaching in Southeast Asia, Africa, Central America and the United States. He passed away in 2013 at the age of 93. When I saw a special recently on TV featuring the Tuskegee Airmen, I was moved to call his wife Adrienne. She answered the phone, and we had a wonderful 30-minute conversation. She was 102 and sharp as a tack.

I met Brigadier General Norman Gaddis when he was a guest speaker for the Tennessee Airports Association Conference in Nashville. Norm was the first Colonel captured by the North Vietnamese on 12 May 1967 when his F-4 was damaged, and he had to eject. He spent almost six years in captivity. As we reminisced, I told him that we were very close together in December 1972 when I was just three miles above him over Hanoi. We became good friends, and he became a sponsor for FLIGHT Foundation. We have kept in touch over the past 20 years, he visited our home when he was inducted into the Tennessee Aviation Hall-of-Fame, and I attended his 100th birthday party at Triangle North Executive Airport in September 2023. What a marvelous gentleman and warrior.

Chapter 16
Best Weekend Ever
(November 2013)

In 2012, I received an offer to be listed in the worldwide Who's Who for company presidents for $800. Well, I am the president of FLIGHT Foundation, a company of two. It was an honor for sure, and a money maker for them, but I couldn't think of how this would help me or the program. I couldn't let it go though, and two weeks later, against my better judgement, signed up — under the guise that I am always shameless about advertising our flying program, and someone might see it and want to give us money.

Rewind a few years and I began to feel bad that I had lost contact with Bob Gomez's family. The Sarasota number was no good and the Military Personnel Center (MPC) locator had no information on them. I seemed to be at a dead end.

Two weeks after paying my $800, I got a call at school from Phillis. She said a Holly Gomez had called and thought you might have been Bob's roommate. I called Holly back and sure enough, I had reconnected with the family. Divine providence again.

Holly is Richard's daughter in law, married to his son Todd. Holly's son Ethan had an assignment in eighth grade to do a project on the Vietnam war. Ethan chose Bob, his great uncle, as his project. Richard, Bob's brother, sent Ethan information on Bob including the letter I had written in 1970 to Art and Kaye when Bob was Missing-In-Action (MIA), Holly googled my name and up popped the info from Who's Who. To have been separated for 43 years and reconnect within two weeks of accepting the Who's Who offer has got to be divine intervention. If the website never gets another hit, it was worth every penny, and much more so, for this one.

I invited the Gomez family to join me at the Tennessee Aviation HOF induction ceremony in Murfreesboro, TN and then attend the Veteran's Day Program at Sullivan South, where I would be the guest speaker. Richard, his wife Suzanne, Holly and Ethan attended. It was surreal. The event was special because my family and friends were there, fellow teachers and administrators, students, and Vietnam buddies.

After the ceremony on Saturday evening, we went back to Unicoi County on Sunday. We got them settled in their motel and then had them over to the house for a visit. On Monday morning we went to TRI-Cities airport, and I flew Holly, Ethan, and Suzanne for a sightseeing tour of the beautiful mountains of east Tennessee.

We were at the Veteran's Day Program that afternoon. I recalled the story of Bob to the audience including my surprise when he showed up at Ubon and was assigned to the same squadron. That we became roommates and several months later were selected to join an elite group of six aircrews out of eighty on the base to fly a specialized forward air controller mission known as Wolf FACs. That we took R&R's together at Pattaya Beach in Thailand, water skiing, snorkeling, and just relaxing for several days. That, when we were not flying, we would play tennis, or take the Baht bus to downtown Ubon to have custom clothes and boots made. And that he was like a brother to me. I recalled the recent reconnection to the family and then introduced them and had them come to the podium.

When I wrote to Art and Kaye in 1970, I asked if I could keep one of Bob's shirts in remembrance of him. We were the same size, and they said sure. I did and started to wear it at Homestead. I quickly realized that if I did this it would end up in the rag pile, so I folded it up and kept it in my dresser.

For this Veteran's Day Program, I thought it would be an appropriate time to take the shirt out of the drawer after 43 years, six months, and 18 days, and wear it one more time. I put it on over my shirt and tie and under my sport jacket. I explained that I did this for two reasons. One because of the subject of the program, and two, because I just wanted them to see that it still fit. Which just proves that if you don't wash things so much, they won't shrink up on you.

At the podium with the family behind me, I explained that it had been my honor to maintain stewardship of this shirt for the past 43 ½ years. But I was not getting any younger, and I thought it appropriate to return it to the Gomez family — specifically to Ethan since it was his project that brought us back together. I told Ethan that this shirt had been worn by a fun-loving, tennis and guitar playing, water-skiing, dedicated, loyal, patriotic, and courageous young flyboy — his great uncle Bob Gomez. I took off my sport coat, took the shirt off and put it on Ethan, explaining that he was now the keeper of the shirt in remembrance of Bob. There was not a dry eye in the house. I was never able to practice this speech at home without getting choked up, but somehow, I got through it during the actual program.

As a teacher myself, I gave Ethan two assignments. The first assignment was long-term — to maintain stewardship of Bob's shirt for the rest of his life, which meant essentially that he couldn't wear it. The second assignment was short-term. I wanted him to wear it, take a family picture, and send that to me. I would keep that picture as a remembrance of Bob for the rest of my life, which I hoped would be a long-term assignment for me. I am so pleased to have that picture in my album.

Austin Moody, one of my former JROTC students and private pilots, came up from Nashville to perform the song "More Than a Name on a Wall" by the Statler Brothers. I wrote a special verse for him to sing about Bob: "I'd like to add a verse for a special friend of mine, we roomed together at Ubon in the fall of '69, we both flew with the Wolf Fac's in the F-4D, I live my life for both of us so all the world can see, Lord Gomez was special, and he meant so much to me..."

After the program, we took about an hour to say goodbye. No one wanted the reunion to end. Finally, we left for home, Holly and Ethan to Mesa, Arizona, and Richard and Suzanne to Atlanta, Georgia. It was another intense, emotional experience. Richard wrote a letter thanking me because this program provided a sense of closure for the family. Bob's remains are still part of the 1200 not returned from Vietnam.

We were privileged to be invited to spend a few days with Richard and Suzanne in Georgia in their second home on a lake. We went out on the lake in their boat, toured the area, and Richard and I enjoyed many games of pool in their home.

Chapter 17
Second Retirement (2013-2024+)

I retired from teaching in June 2013. This was a very difficult decision. I really enjoyed my job and loved working with the kids. In addition to all the normal talents needed for being a good teacher, two things stood out to me as the only way to survive 22 years in the classroom — forgiving and forgetting. Kids will drive you crazy if you don't have some short-term memory loss. Each day you come to work you have to come with a clean slate. Otherwise, things will pile up continuously. Another challenge is that you have kids in your class for four years — just like an athletic coach or band director. I can't tell you how many times a parent would come and tell me I couldn't retire until their cadet had graduated. It truly was a family atmosphere. I tried to comply with those requests for a few years, but eventually, I had to pull the plug. You can't make everybody happy, or you could never retire. The real challenge was that, as the flying program became more successful, I was spending more time at the airport, and Don Shawver was spending way too much time in the classroom. He needed relief. The best option was for me to retire, keep my flying job, and hire another instructor for the classroom.

The Air Force had paid me to wear the uniform for 50 years, from 1963 until 2013. I thought that was a nice round number to leave on. I felt I had given the Academy and the Air Force their money's worth.

I was hired by the Sullivan County Director of Schools in 2014 to implement flight programs in other schools in Sullivan County and to keep flying students. After that year I was hired as a flight coach for $1,000 a year. This was important to me so that I would remain an insider, a member of the school system — the magic bullet.

In 2014, we took on the project of making a FLIGHT Foundation calenda for the 2015 year. Diane Copas, mom of one of my AFJROTC students for three years until I retired and one of my solo students, was a professional photographer and had done many photo shoots for JROTC and FLIGHT Foundation in the past. We had several sessions at the Greeneville Municipal Airport, where students would dress up and she would take pictures of them around the airplane performing normal preflight duties in their gowns and suits. The picture of me in the tuxedo next to the Cessna-152 was taken at one of those sessions.

The calendar featured a different solo student for each month. It was spectacular, and the students and their families were excited and would have a memento for the rest of their lives. The idea was for this to be a fundraiser. Not so much. Calendars were outdated in 2015 and most of the sales were to the 12 students and their circle of family and friends. It basically paid for itself. In addition to the calendar photos, we took some James Bond poses which makes me smile even to this day. When I look at all the photos, I am grateful for Diane and the excitement generated by making the calendar.

Two years later. Sullivan County decided they had too much of a good thing and no longer wanted the flight program. WTFO? I was immediately hired by the Greene County school system to be their flight coach, where I am still employed today. The numbers just keep adding up. We are now (Aug '24) over 13,200 students flown on flight orientation program (FOP) flights, called discovery or introductory flights by other organizations such as Civil Air Patrol (CAP) and the Experimental Aircraft Association (EAA), 292 students soloed, and 47 private pilots. In today's market, the orientation flights went from free to a $10 donation per student, solo scholarships are $1000 and private pilot scholarships are $4000 ($5000 total). On 16 June 2023, I flew my 10,000[th] FOP student. We had a special ceremony at the Greeneville Municipal Airport with state and local dignitaries attending, and it was captured by the local newspaper (the Greeneville Sun) and WJHL-TV (CBS). I am blessed to be able to do this and feel as enthusiastic about going to the airport today as I did 56 years ago. I just walk to the airplane a little slower.

Ever since I visited the family burial plot at Ashland Cemetery in Carlisle, Pennsylvania in 2006, I was struck by the fact that my grandfather's gravestone was not there. The Ewing brothers had known my grandparents for years along with the Faber's (Grace Faber was Dedad's sister.) There were two large headstones, one with Faber and one with Powley. The individual burial plots were flat marble stones for each family member placed in front of the headstone. The cemetery was now run by the son of these two gentlemen, Steve Ewing. It was not until 2012 that I called Steve to inquire as to why my grandfather did not have a marble stone. Steve checked the records and could find nothing about him being buried there.

Several years went by and I confirmed with my uncle, who had attended the funeral in Towson, Maryland, and made the trip to Carlisle, PA for the internment. You wouldn't forget a two-hour funeral procession. In subsequent calls to Steve, I told him I was pretty sure he was buried there and probably in the family plot. We were both perplexed and a little confused by the issue. Somehow, he found an old record that showed one burial plot on the other side of the road going by our headstones. He took a rod and discovered the coffin on that side of the road. We were elated that the mystery had been solved. My brother Ken and I split the cost of the marker, and we were happy to solve the mystery and add Edgar Powley's marker to the rest of the family in 2021. Persistence again paid off.

My brother Ken and sister-in-law Penny (Lilly-Seed) invited Phillis and me to visit them again on Anna Marie Island on Florida's Gulf Coast the last week in January 2014. We were excited to do this because we had previously done so a decade ago. Ken and Penny had rented a house on the island for a month, and we went down to spend a week with them.

My trip coordinator, Phillis, made the plane and car reservations. When we got to Orlando, Sanford I went to the rental car desk and found out that the car was reserved at Orlando International Airport. Phillis did not know that Orlando had two airports. Fortunately, they had one car left — a Ford Mustang. We set out around 11:30 in the evening and arrived on the island around 2 am. The speed limit on the island was 15 and I was doing 25. Phillis was having a fit saying I was speeding and was going to get a ticket. I could walk faster than I was driving, and I was the only one on a road on the entire island. Just then, blue flashing lights appeared behind us. I pulled over to Phillis' *I told you so*. The cop came up and looked in and Phillis started laughing. She said I bet you thought we were kids on spring break and he said yes. He started laughing also and let the senior citizens go.

We got to bed around 3 am and when we got up around 9 the next morning, Ken asked if I wanted to take a bike ride to a great breakfast restaurant. I said sure. Ken is a biking guru, having peddled across the country twice. As we started out, I asked how far to the restaurant. Twenty-six miles he says. Saay whaaat? Now I can bike with the best of them as long as I don't have to sit on the seat. You would think that since bike riding started in 1817, they could make a seat that would be comfortable. Not possible. The meal was great, but no restaurant is worth a 52-mile round trip bike ride.

On the way back we had a flat tire. No problem. The girls had the van with all the support equipment. They were tasked with immediately responding to our call for help. Hard to do when you are at the mall and don't answer your damn phones. We set out walking our bikes and asking at different houses if they had a bicycle pump. No such luck. Did I mention that Florida is warm all year long? We waited three hours to get rescued. I don't want to go back to that restaurant ever again.

Back to the original story. Phillis and I go to the airport before the sun comes up, I get the bags out, and Phillis comes around to the back of the car, hands me a ticket, and tells me I'm going by myself. What? She drives off and I am left standing in the road in the dark with my bags wondering what just happened.

I checked in to go to Atlanta and then Sarasota. I called Phillis and asked what was going on. She said, "I think you and your brother are going out of the country." I said I didn't have my passport. She said she put it in my luggage. Liar.

When I got to Sarasota, Ken met me at baggage claim. He said we had no time to wait for my luggage, so we ran through the airport to an exit where he handed me a box and told me to get on the bus. It read Baltimore Orioles Dream Camp. What? Ken went back to get my bag which had my gloves in them, and tennis racquets for my supposed Anna Marie Island vacation.

The bus took us to the Orioles spring training facility in Sarasota. Ken had paid for my week's stay. The box contained a new pair of baseball cleats. We had lockers with uniforms with our names on them. That Sunday afternoon we had practice so the coaches could get their draft picks in order. I borrowed a glove from a fellow camper. I was drafted on a team managed by ex-Oriole's catcher Chris Hoiles and coached by ex-Orioles pitcher Dave Johnson. There were six teams, and all were managed and coached by ex-Oriole major leaguers. I knew all of them.

This was truly a dream. We played two seven-inning games a day. We lost both games on Monday. I started the first game on Tuesday. I had not pitched since 1969. But I had played sports my entire life including fast and slow-pitch softball, flag football, and tennis. To attend the camp, you had to be over 30 and I was the fifth oldest camper at 68. I pitched the first three innings on Tuesday morning, which was the max allowed. By the second inning Chris Hoiles was calling me Cy Young. Now that's high cotton.

We won that game and would go on to win every other game and win the Championship. Holy Cow! My record for the camp was 1-0 with a 0.00 ERA. We got pictures with the pros, bought memorabilia, hung out with these guys to hear all sorts of wild stories about Earl Weaver and all the antics that went on. We had our last game Saturday morning that we had to win to get into the championship game. The camp was supposed to end Friday, but due to rain we had to play speed-up games Saturday morning — six innings and every batter had a 1-1 count when they stepped in the batter's box. We were down 4-1 in the bottom of the sixth inning. I was the lead-off batter. I took the first pitch which was a strike and already I had a 1-2 count. I was not going to strike out or trust the ump to make a close call in my favor. The next pitch was well outside (I am a right-handed batter), but I put the barrel of the bat on it and drove it over the first baseman's head for a lead-off single.

I ended up scoring to make it 4-2, we had the bases loaded with two out, and one of our young studs at the plate. He hit a deep fly ball over the left fielder's head and cleared the bases with a triple. We won 5-4. You would have thought we just won the World Series. When we got back in the locker room after the game, the catcher for the opposing team was saying that the ball I hit was a foot off the plate (I thought six inches max) and Chris Hoiles said that was great hitting. High cotton again. If I had made an out, we would have never gotten to the bases loaded situation with two outs.

Part of the Dream Camp experience is that you get to play in Camden Yards that same year in Baltimore when the Orioles are on the road. We played the championship game there in June and won 16-4. I got to pitch, play third base and left field, and went 2-4. It just doesn't get any better than that. A championship at 14 and at 68. I forgive Phillis and Ken for deceiving me.

The other part of the experience is that you can play any year at Cooperstown when they hold the camp. I went several years later and got to pitch, play second base, and bat on Doubleday Field. That's also high cotton.

The next year in December 2015, Phillis and I became famous in our little town of Unicoi. I played on the local TRI-Cities slow-pitch over 65 softball team for several years. This is where Phillis takes over as she threw me under the bus, deservedly, and told the story to The Erwin Record, published on 15 Dev 2015, entitled "Bargain tree has costly price tag."

"One of the members of the team had a Christmas tree farm. This gentleman offered his teammates a live Christmas tree any size, for $20. With the 'bargain' light flashing in my husband's brain, he said 'Sure, I'll take the tallest one you've got'.

"The day came to get the tree, so we drove out in Bill's pickup truck to get his $20 buy. Well, it was 16 feet high and took three people to lug it into the back of the pickup. We begged and borrowed banners to tie the end jutting out and somehow got home in one piece.

"What do you do with a 16-foot tree? First, I went to Walmart and bought another $70 worth of lights. Now a $90 tree. Then Bill hired two young men to help him trim the top and bottom and somehow get it into the house, straighten it up, and set it in the stand. Another $200, so we now have a huge $290 tree.

With that finally done, it was time to cut the rope holding it closed. With a giant 'tharrump' the tree sprang open. Has anyone seen Chevy Chase's 'Christmas Vacation movie? I fully expected a squirrel to jump out! Furniture tumbled forward, every window (including the one in the ceiling) was blocked, and my nice big living room was now the size of a postage stamp. I had to move all the furniture to the far wall because of the size of the tree.

So, the last 10 days have been spent putting on lights and the angel on top of the tree with two 12-foot ladders on opposite sides of the tree, ornaments and vacuuming up pine needles. The dog had helped by pulling off the ornaments she didn't like, so we have replaced those. The circuit breaker is now working all right. And I have learned a very good lesson about men and bargains. I can hardly wait to see how much this beauty is going to cost in time and money to get it out of here come New Year! But for now, have a Merry Christmas."

After that shot across the bow, I had to do a follow-up which was published on 20 Jan 2016 in The Erwin Record entitled "Bargain tree leaves Unicoi home with memories, needles."

"Since my wife Phillis threw me under the bus with her 'story' about my bargain Christmas tree, I thought I would follow up with how the tree came down — since everyone in the community wanted her to write about it. But I can't afford anymore tire tracks on my body.

"She was 'anxious,' 'insistent,' whatever, about getting that tree down pronto. So, I 'hired' my normal Saturday worker to help me take it down, now that my right hand was strong enough for me to do my share. Phillis spent several days taking the decorations off — quicker that putting them up since the 'right spot' had already been chosen. I helped take the lower lights off, got the eight-foot ladder and took the decorations off as high as I could reach — which was about four feet from the top.

"That Saturday I cut the top of the tree off — only problem was when I cut the top off, I found the tree had branched and there were two tops. Having taken 'both' tops off we could now take the lights and decorations off the top of the tree.

"We then trimmed the bottom branches off creating the effect of a palm tree. (Remember when we put it in the house it was bundled.) We were then ready to release it from the stand and take it outside. It fit 'perfectly' out the door and over the railing — leaving behind a mere 200,000 needles. Not to worry. A dustpan, broom, and the vacuum took care of the rest. The carpet cleaners normally come in six months or so. Voila — a room restored to normalcy — and all in under two hours (it would have been two days if Phillis had written this — but much more exciting.)

The tree was placed in the woods for the critters to hide in, so the planet is in good shape. We keep finding ornaments in the woods. It is just disappointing to me that Easter does not have a 'tree' associated with the holiday. I could get a really large bunny."

There. Enough said.

Chapter 18
Fishing
(1973-present)

Our fishing adventures started, as I mentioned, at Eglin AFB in 1973 at the Pendery's lakes. It continued through Fort Worth, Texas on Benbrook, and even to Hawaii, fishing for tilapia in some of the small lakes in central Oahu.

The fishing tradition dates back to my great-grandfather, John C. Powley, who took out his last fishing license at the age of 90 in 1934. He was recognized as the oldest fisherman in Cumberland County, Pennsylvania.

Bob and Bill went to high school in Fort Worth and stayed there to find jobs and raise their families. I would visit them throughout the decades that followed. and we would always have a fishing trip as one of the main events of the visit.

We tried several lakes and one of the most popular at that time was Lake Fork — a reservoir impounded by the Lake Fork Dam in 1980. We started fishing there in the early nineties. One trip is memorable because before the trip Bill bought a new rod and reel. We set out in Bob's boat and headed for an open area over a grass flat. There are only 8 million good looking fishing spots around the lake, and we knew none of them. In this case we got lucky. On Bill's first cast with his new rod and reel he caught a seven-pound largemouth bass. It was surreal. We were all ecstatic. Unfortunately, the euphoria wore off quickly as that was the only fish we caught all day. That's why it's called fishing and not catching, but we would turn the tables on the fish in the upcoming years.

One of Bob's friends from work knew a place to fish in Aubrey, Texas, about an hour and a half north of Dallas-Fort Worth. In his honor, we call it Grayson's pond. It is an old rock quarry that filled up with water. Over the years, the hydrilla filled the pond and was pretty much untouched or managed for years.

Our first trip there was like being a kid in a candy store. This was catching at its best. If you made a cast with any lure, and didn't get a strike on two consecutive casts, you would be having a bad day. I like to fish top-water lures, where the fish strikes are spectacular because you can see them. Normally, these lures are more effective in the early morning and late evening. I used them all day and caught fish all day long. What fun. Many times, all three of us would have a fish on. On one cast I caught two fish on the top water lure. We released all the fish. By the end of the day, my thumb would be raw and shredded by lipping the bass to lift them into the boat and take the hook out to release them. At this point, I was hoping for a long-distance release before they got to the boat. We made several trips to this hot spot over the span of a decade. On our most memorable trip, we caught 250 bass in about six hours. Now that will spoil you big-time for fishing.

There was a dry spell for many years. I decided I wasn't getting any younger, so it was time to organize some "special" fishing adventures to include all the Powley boys — my brother Ken, his son Jonathan, my two boys and Bob's son, Vincent. The first adventure was to the Louisiana bayou in Belle Chase, south of New Orleans in September 2016. We hired guides for the two days of fishing for redfish, speckled trout, and drum. This was fishing, not catching. We picked the absolute worst time to go, according to the guides, just because the weather and water conditions were on the downturn. As our family can attest, we can shut down the best fishing holes in an instant. However, in our defense, we had to pick a time when all six of us could get off work, which was a challenge.

The next adventure was three years later in September 2019. September is the time for us, because Jonathan works at Yankee stadium and we have to wait until baseball season is over for him to join us. My friend Tom Reeves has been fishing lakes in Canada just north of International Falls, Minnesota for over 40 years. He had invited me to go along on one of his trips, but I opted to use this as an opportunity to plan another guy's trip. He provided all the expertise for us to make our first venture to Lake Kiskutena a memorable and pleasant one.

Lake Kishkutena is a beautiful remote lake, accessible only by float plane. I drove from Unico, Tennessee to meet Ken and Jonathan, coming from Mountain Top, Pennsylvania, at my sister Barb's house in Cincinnati, Ohio. We drove to International Falls together, taking the food and fishing gear in Ken's vehicle. Bob, Bill, and Vincent flew to International Falls from Fort Worth, Texas.

We met Tom and his crew in International Falls, crossed the border, and drove about two hours to Nestor Falls, where we spent the night. The next morning, we flew in a de Havilland Beaver to our cabin on the lake. The pilot dropped us off and wished us good luck. Hopefully we would all be alive when he stopped back in a week to pick us up.

Again, we managed to shut down the fishing in the lake. Tom said it was probably the worst year of fishing he had seen in the 40 plus years he had been fishing in Canada. Great, just what we were hoping for. Something about an unusually hot August that had killed most of the grasses in the honey holes along the banks. The only thing to do there for the week was to fish, so we worked hard at it. We did catch a lot of fish, but we didn't slay 'em like we had hoped to. We had the privilege of seeing four beautiful and majestic bald eagles who lived less than a hundred yards from us. We would take the fish remains, after we had filleted them, to a rock next to the water and watch as the eagles came in and either ate them there or took them away. It was magnificent and breathtaking. Bob said that, as he was walking a trail around the little island we were on, an eagle swooped over him at about ten feet, and he thought it was an airplane.

One of the more remarkable things about our stay at Kishkutena, was that no one ever had to tell anybody what to do. The guys just did whatever had to be done which included keeping the generators filled with gas to keep some lights on after dark and recharging the batteries for the trolling motors, cleaning the fish, grilling, cooking, cleaning, etc. We ate every bit of food in the large Yeti cooler Food City filled and packed with dry ice, in addition to two very fresh fish dinners.

We all survived and got picked up to head home. It was the first time any of us had been in a float plane. They used a Beaver and a Cessna 206 to get the whole group in and out.

I got my brother back for punking me into going to the Orioles dream camp. I had him come down to Unicoi to go striped bass fishing on Boone Lake about 30 minutes from us. Phillis and I had gone out years before with a guide and caught some really nice fish. At the time she texted her son, Cord, and told him we were going after strippers instead of stripers. Cord texted back telling her to make sure we had a lot of one-dollar bills. She didn't get it. Finally, I had to explain it to her. She never asked how I knew.

The fishing trip for Ken was a partial ruse, because when he got here, I put him in my truck and we started driving to South Carolina. Now it was his turn to wonder and ask questions. When we got to our motel in Greenville, the TV stations were there, and a crowd was gathering. I didn't know they knew we were coming. Turns out they didn't. We were staying in the same hotel as the Auburn football team for a game the next day against South Carolina.

The next morning, we got up and headed for the BMW driving school. If you own a BMW, the school is free. If you didn't, not so much. We didn't. But we had a grand time. A few minutes of ground school and then out to the cars.

Our first event was the skid pad, a slick marble-like circular pad with water sprayed on it. There were three in the car with the instructor, and we all took turns at the wheel. You would intentionally put yourself into a skid and then try to recover. Looked pretty simple. Not so fast. There were two cars on the pad at one time, 180 degrees apart from each other. They drilled the recovery procedure into us, not that we did it perfect that day, but I still remember CPR — correct, pause, recover.

After that, everyone had their own car with a walkie talkie to hear the instructor. We had several different courses that we ran for time. The last training course was a small oval racetrack that was damp at several places. Two cars would start opposite each other midway down the straight away and see who could gain on the other. It only lasted a minute. I was in the finals and lost to a 30-year younger pilot.

The last training course was for everyone at the same time. We would be spaced apart during the start and then go for it. There was one straight away about a quarter of a mile long. When you came out of the turn you would floor it, accelerate to over 100 miles an hour, stomp on the brakes to make a hairpin left turn, then accelerate and brake again. The whole time it seemed like it was full throttle or full brake.

The last event of the day was scary. Three of us got in a car with a professional driver and they took a road course at full speed. Well, how easy is that. Just keep the accelerator to the floor and skid around all the turns with the wheels smoking and your passengers screaming. At least they were having a fun time. Now I know why the course is so expensive. They must go through a hundred tires in a day.

When we got back home, we went striper fishing. It was cold and we about froze to death, but we did catch a few — very few.

Chapter 19
Florence (Nanny) Powley (1898-1996)
and Herb (1918-1943)

It is amazing to think of the changes Nanny lived through being born in 1898. Let me just mention a few events. President's William McKinley, Teddy Roosevelt, William Taft, Woodrow Wilson, Warren Harding, Calvin Coolidge, Herbert Hoover, FDR, the Wright brothers, Kitty Hawk, the airplane, WWI, the great depression, WWII, Korea, Vietnam, Desert Storm, Afghanistan, the Model-T Ford, the television, space travel, Alan Shepherd, Neil Armstrong, walking on the moon, computers, every comfort we have in our homes, air-conditioning, heating, the ratification of the treaty of the Spanish-American war of 1898. What do all these events have in common? Nan was there for all of them.

When Nanny was in her nineties, I had the good sense to have her record on cassette tapes some of the family history and stories. Sadly, it was not until after she passed that I sat down and transcribed those stories on the computer. In the process of transcribing, Nan mentioned that she had only one regret in her life, that Herb had not graduated from Springfield College. He was the first senior to leave Springfield College after war was declared, just three months before graduation, to join the Army Air Forces. I decided to see if I could do something about that.

I contacted Damon Markiewicz, head of Media Relations, at the college at the college and explained the situation. To my delight, they were very supportive. In the process of pursuing this goal, I received copies from the archives of all the school newspapers that had articles on Herb Powley. He was in most of them, either for sports — varsity soccer, ice hockey, lacrosse — or performances by his band, the Springfield Dons - he was the drummer - at many of the college dances. He also served on the Springfield College Student Council, was one of 10 seniors selected for inclusion in the Who's Who magazine for American Colleges and Universities for the 1941-1942 school year and was a member of the Varsity Club.

The process started in 2017 and was completed in only six months. Springfield College President, Dr. Mary-Beth Cooper, signed the diploma which has an effective date of 22 May 1942 — Herb's original graduation date had he remained in college. Mary-Beth sent me a heartwarming letter on 16 Apr 2018, stating "Learning about Herb, it was clear that he embodied the commitment and promise of a Springfield College graduate and lived a life in concert with our Humanics tradition. His achievement in academics, athletics, music, community service, and his ultimate sacrifice for his countrymen are commendable. We are proud to call him one of our own."

She concluded with "I know that you and your family will appreciate the knowledge that his academic accomplishment has been rewarded and marked in history for all to know." We certainly do appreciate this honor for Herbert Frank Powley. I am honored to be named after him and to carry on his legacy as a pilot. I was proud to be the first in our family to be a college graduate. Now, 82 years later, I am even more proud to be the second in our family to be a college graduate.

One of my own personal regrets is that I did not accomplish this sooner so Nanny could witness it. Somehow, I hope that she is aware that her oldest son is a college graduate.

I have had many conversations with President Cooper since she sent me that letter which accompanied the diploma. I will be eternally grateful for her efforts to make the diploma a reality. The man behind the scenes in the registrar's office was Keith Ingalls. He is the one I contacted first and was willing to help me out. He provided all the information and made this a reality. He included another heartwarming letter with the diploma. He stated:" Through our conversations, emails and the journey of digging into the past and realizing that there are no small parts to what we do, I have felt the positive of the impact we have on each other, the reinforcement of the purposes that we all have, as common or different as they may be."

"Again, on a personal note, it has been very fulfilling to put a face and a story behind what has been, until now, just a name on a plaque. My staff have shared in this with me as I have kept them updated with each of our conversations and emails. I think it serves as a wonderful reminder that each student is important, each interaction can have an impact, and that there is no telling today how the life and path of that student may turn out."

"Your uncle had a very positive impact on Springfield College while a student here, and some 75 plus years later, that impact has been resurrected and continues to remind people here of who and what we are, the students that we attract, nurture and send back out into the world to serve others."

"Your uncle was a special person, and as I mentioned, I think that you have a bond, and much more in common with him than you may ever come to realize. It has been an honor to assist with collecting and sharing information with you on his time here at Springfield College. I also appreciate the information that you have shared with me."

One of the outcomes of this effort was that the college will research others who attended but did not graduate, due to their military service, to give their families a diploma even if they do not request it. Now that brings tears to my eyes. I plan to visit Springfield, Massachusetts as a guest of Mary-Beth and see the college that my uncle Herb attended, and to walk on the lacrosse fields that he played on with the same sticks that I used at the Air Force Academy 25 years later.

Think about the response of Springfield College to my request, requiring them to do a lot of extra work, which was certainly not required. How many times have requests for something like this gotten a response like "That's not our job" or "We don't have time" or "We can't help you," or a myriad of other excuses to not help. This should be the standard for anyone calling themselves a service organization. And look at the positive results for everyone involved. I can never thank you enough.

I have so much love and affection for my grandmother. One thing I will never forget about her is that she always put money in my hand when I visited her as we were leaving. This started from the time I can remember, maybe 6 or 7 and continued until she passed away in 1996 and I was 51 years old. The only thing that changed was that she kept up with inflation. Instead of getting a quarter she would give me $20. I tried to tell her 30 years before she passed that it was not necessary. Apparently, it was to her, and she enjoyed it so much that I never mentioned it again.

I was inspired to write a poem about her called *Grandmothers*.

> *Grandmothers are wonderful.*
> *They know how to share*

Love's precious gift of grace
Expressed in tender care.

They've outgrown all selfishness,
And striving to be known.
They comfort and support us,
Whenever we feel alone.

They have a gentle presence.
And speak in softened tones.
They live in secret places,
Close to heavenly homes.

As we stumble through life's roadblocks
They encourage us on our way.
They never seem to criticize,
But know just what to say.

They watch us with great patience.
At our work and at our play.
They fill our lives with hope,
Leading us to a brighter day.

Mothers, wives, and sisters,
Fathers, husbands, brothers,
Wouldn't the world be blest,
If all were just grandmothers.

When I spoke at Nanny's funeral, I closed with the refrain from a song by Collin Raye called "If You Get There Before I Do," about a note a grandma wrote to her husband. I had thought about that song in relation to Nanny and Dedad, and to Nan and myself. It goes like this: "If you get there before I do, don't give up on me. I'll meet you when my chores are through, I don't know how long I'll be but I'm not going to let you down, Nanny, wait and see. And between now and then, until I see you again, I'll be lovin' you, love me."

Chapter 20
Ralph Hood
(2002-2022)

In 2002, I met Ralph Hood in Murfreesboro, Tennessee. He was the guest speaker at the annual Tennessee Aviation Association (TAA) airport's conference in March. He was a pilot, aircraft salesman, and insurance agent. He delivered airplanes around the country to customers. He had a knack for storytelling. Being from Brunswick, Georgia he had a funny accent. He appeared on the Oprah Winfrey show as a stand in for Lewis Grizzard. After the show, Oprah said he was a funny man. That is high cotton.

Ralph was inducted into the Alabama Aviation HOF as the Aviation Humorist. When you read his introduction in the program you were laughing before he ever uttered a word. He mentioned that he had spoken in all 50 states and two foreign countries- Canada and Washington DC.

One of his stories was about delivering an airplane in west Texas. The weather was deteriorating, he was lost, everything was flat and looked the same, and he was low on fuel. He decided to follow a road, sure it would lead him to a gas station. Sure enough, it did. He landed on the road and taxied to the pump. The attendant came out and Ralph told him to fill 'er up while he went to the bathroom. Upon returning he said to the attendant," guess you don't see too many airplanes stop by here." The attendant said," nope, most of 'em land across the street at the airport." Funny stuff. You can't forget that.

About a decade later, Ralph and his wife Gail moved to Erwin, TN. I couldn't believe my good luck. Just having a cup of coffee with Ralph or going to a Kiwanis meeting was a treat. I had the "pleasure" of driving him to Oshkosh with Fain Bennett to make a speech up there. He never shut up for the entire 17-hour trip up and back. We didn't mind. He was a hoot. He wrote a book *The Truth and Other Lies*, a compilation of newspaper columns he wrote for decades. He has a million stories if not more.

Ralph is the one who nominated me for the Flight Instructor HOF (FIHOF) several years ago. He passed away last year, but Fain Bennett picked up the ball and used Ralph's letter again this year for the nomination. This year we got it. I hope Ralph knows. If you never heard him speak, you missed something special. Gail is special also.

I was in the briefing room at the Greeneville Municipal Airport in between flights when John Niehaus and Paul Preidecker called from NAFI (National Association of Flight Instructors). They informed me that I had been selected as the 2023 inductee into the FIHOF. Holy cow! This is high cotton. One instructor in the entire nation. I asked one of the selection committee members what they had been drinking when they made the selection. He laughed. But he said I deserved it. I'll take it. Thank you.

I accepted the invitation to go to Oshkosh and receive the award on the morning of 27 July in the NAFI tent at 0800. They made me feel like a rock star. Beth Stanton set it up and Bob Meder drove Beth, my sister, and me right to the tent at 0630 to avoid all the traffic and parking hassles. Thank you. Little stress. I met some old friends there and met some new ones that I had only talked to on the phone. One was Chuck Ahearn, President of The Ray Foundation, who had been providing matching grants for three years. There were former students and soon to be students from the Civil Air Patrol (CAP) contingent from Greeneville at Oshkosh for a drone contest.

I only had five minutes to speak but stretched it into seven. I mentioned Bob Gomez, Bill Delaplane, and told them the stories of Chuck Dragich and Richard Little. I knew they would remember stories instead of speeches — a lesson I took from Ralph Hood, whom I also mentioned. I told them the story of the one vote and how it made a difference and that was why I was receiving this award today. I told them that in grade school we were shown that you can't put a square peg in a round hole. Not true. You can. You just have to beat the crap out of it, like driving 80 miles round trip to the airport every time you fly for 30 years.

A quote attributed to Sir Winston Churchill states: "To each there comes in their lifetime a special moment when they are figuratively tapped on the shoulder and offered the chance to do a very special thing, unique to them and fitted to their talents. What a tragedy if that moment finds them unprepared or unqualified for that which could have been their finest hour." I am so grateful that I was prepared and qualified. Professionally, this was my finest hour.

My goal is to keep beating the crap out of it as long as the good Lord is willing.

Epilogue

I wrote this book in 40 hours, with a pen and paper. It had been rattling around in my head for a decade or so and there was no time for it to spill out. Just weeks after my FIHOF induction ceremony, Phillis and I went to Cincinnati, Ohio to dog sit Cord's new puppy. He had been working from home, but now had to go in to work for 10 hours a day for a week of training.

Max, a border collie, is a cute and energetic puppy. But, cooped up with him all day gave me time to write. What I wrote from start to finish is just how it came out of my head.

I could tell twice as many stories (I actually had to add many of them to make the book large enough to be published), but I wanted to keep it short and sweet, so it wouldn't be laborious. Maybe the next 40 hours I have to dog sit, I can write volume II.

I have a saying that I kept on my desk for decades. It was printed with the F-16 as the backdrop. "Nothing in the world can take the place of Persistence. Talent will not; nothing is more common than unsuccessful men with talent. Genius will not; unrewarded genius is almost a proverb. Education will not; the world is full of educated derelicts. Persistence and determination alone are omnipotent."

If I am in a room with others, I am not the smartest, not the dumbest, not the best looking, not the best dressed, not the cunningest, not the tallest, not the biggest or the smallest, but I am the most persistent SOB in the room. I hope this story bears that out to some degree.

Our family has a history of military service for five generations from the Civil War, my great-grandfather John C, Powley, WWI, my grandfather and his brother Herbert, WWII, my uncle Herbert and my dad (Aviation Cadets), Vietnam, me, to my son Billy in the 10th Mountain Infantry in Somalia and Haiti. I am the only career military member.

There were two men standing in front of St. Peter trying to get into heaven. The first gave St. Peter his name, was wearing a leather jacket, jeans, cowboy boots and aviator glasses, and said he had been an airline pilot for 35 years. St. Peter looked him up, said here you are, come on in, and gave him a silk robe and gold staff. The second gentleman stepped up, gave St. Peter his name and told him he had been a preacher for 43 years. St. Peter looked him up, said here you are, come on in, and gave him a cloth robe and wooden staff. While appreciative to get in, he asked why the pilot had gotten the better stuff. St. Peter said, Padre, up here we base everything on results. When you preached, people slept. When he flew, people prayed.

I am here today because people have been praying for me for 56 years of flying.

A toast: To we few, we happy few, we band of brothers. Here, Here.

May God bless you and the United States of America.

Glossary of Terms

AAA — Anti-Aircraft Artillery (Flack)

ABCCC — Airborne Command and Control Center

AF — Air Force

AFCMD — Air Force Contract Management Division

AFJROTC — Air Force Reserve Officer Training Corp

AFPRO — Air Force Plant Representative Office

AFSC — Air Force Systems Command

AGL — Above Ground Level

AMRAAM — Advanced Medium Range Air-to-Air Missile

ATC — Air Traffic Control

ATP — Acceptance Test Procedures

BDU — Battle Dress Uniform

CAP — Civil Air Patrol

CBU — Cluster Bomb Unit

CINC — Commander-in-Chief

DMZ — Demilitarized Zone

EAA — Experimental Aircraft Association

ERA — Earned Run Average

FAA — Federal Aviation Administration

FIHOF — Flight Instructor Hall of Fame

FOP — Flight Orientation Program

FUF — Fellow Up Front

HOF — Hall of Fame

HUD — Head-Up Display

JROTC — Junior Reserve Officer Training Corp

MIA — Missing in Action

MPC — Military Personnel Center

MRE — Meals Ready to Eat

NAFI — National Association of Flight Instructors

NKP — Nakhon Phanom Royal Thai Air Force Base

OER — Officer Evaluation Report

PACAF — Pacific Air Forces

PCS — Permanent Change of Station

R & R — Rest and Recuperation/Relaxation

RBG — Researched Bible Guide

RHAW — Radar Homing and Warning

RTU — Replacement Training Unit

SAR — Search and Rescue

SPO — System Program Office

TAA — Tennessee Airports Association

TAC — Tactical Air Command

TAWC — Tactical Air Warfare Center

TDY — Temporary Duty

TFS — Tactical Fighter Squadron

TFW — Tactical Fighter Wing

USAFA — United States Air Force Academy

USTA — United States Tennis Association

VA — Veterans Administration

WAG — Wild Ass Guess

WSMR — White Sands Missile Range

WTFO = What The Heck Over

About The Author

Bill Powley is blessed to have grown up in a home with two parents from the greatest generation — a working father and stay at home mother. He is equally blessed to have a loving and supportive wife, Phillis, who has allowed him to have the stories presented in this book. Together they have three sons, Bob (wife Katie), Cord, and Bill (wife Gina) and four grandchildren, Vincent, Connor, Hannah, and Lilly. Their two current dogs are Pualani, a nine-year-old Rottweiler, and Sundance, a one-year-old Golden Retriever. They live in the beautiful mountains of East Tennessee in the town of Unicoi, where they enjoy their 10 acres of pastures, woods, barn, ponds, gardens, flower beds, raising quail and fish. Also included are mowing, weeding, mending fences, trimming, and felling trees, and repairing things ad nauseam. He will be forever grateful for his religious upbringing and the morals instilled in him at home, church, and school. One of the most important of these was to never look down on another person, regardless of their station in life, but to treat everyone with kindness and respect.